*The
Sherlock Holmes
Handbook*

THE
SHERLOCK HOLMES HANDBOOK

*The Methods and Mysteries
of the World's Greatest Detective*

BY RANSOM RIGGS
ILLUSTRATIONS BY EUGENE SMITH

QUIRK BOOKS
PHILADELPHIA

Library of Congress Cataloging in Publication Number: 2009924887

ISBN: 978-1-59474-429-7

Printed in China

Typeset in Bembo and Bodoni
Designed by Doogie Horner
Illustrations by Eugene Smith
Production management by John J. McGurk

Distributed in North America by Chronicle Books
680 Second Street
San Francisco, CA 94107

10 9 8 7 6 5 4 3 2 1

Quirk Books
215 Church Street
Philadelphia, PA 19106
www.irreference.com
www.quirkbooks.com

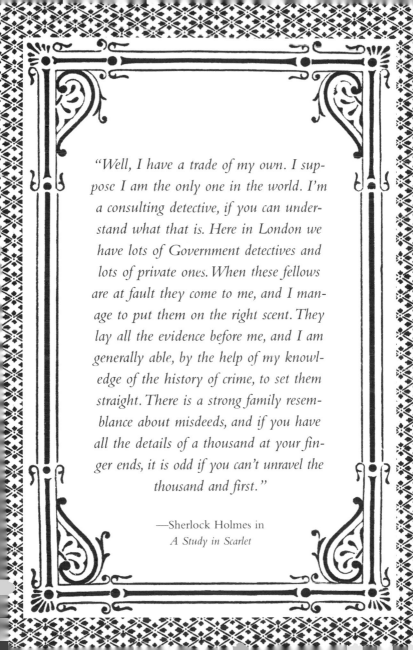

"Well, I have a trade of my own. I suppose I am the only one in the world. I'm a consulting detective, if you can understand what that is. Here in London we have lots of Government detectives and lots of private ones. When these fellows are at fault they come to me, and I manage to put them on the right scent. They lay all the evidence before me, and I am generally able, by the help of my knowledge of the history of crime, to set them straight. There is a strong family resemblance about misdeeds, and if you have all the details of a thousand at your finger ends, it is odd if you can't unravel the thousand and first."

—Sherlock Holmes in
A Study in Scarlet

❖ TABLE OF CONTENTS ❖

Introduction

*"My name is Sherlock Holmes. It is my business to
know what other people don't know."*
—"The Adventure of the Blue Carbuncle"

 midst the vast breadth of works written about Sherlock
Holmes, the volume which you hold in your hands is
unique. It seeks both to instruct the aspiring investigator
in the ways of the master and to serve as an entrée for the casual
reader into the fascinating milieu, brilliant methods, and unortho-
dox habits of the world's most famous consulting detective.

Some readers may wonder, given the volume of material on
Sherlock Holmes already extant, why another book is warranted;
there were fictional detectives before him, after all, and have been
countless since—so, *why Holmes?* The answer may help to illumi-
nate why the fifty-six short stories in which he appears have never
been out of print. His character is a prototype that has often been
imitated but never improved upon and whose legendary methods

of logical deduction are studied by real-world investigators to this day. With Sherlock Holmes, Arthur Conan Doyle brought the detective story into the modern era, perfected the crime thriller, and even helped birth the spy genre in several WWI-era stories in which Holmes protects British secrets from foreign enemies and acts as a double agent. The contemporary police procedurals which now clog our airwaves owe their existence to Sherlock Holmes, and the great bulk of "buddy cop" movies trade upon a model established by Holmes and Watson. More than simply influential, Sherlock Holmes has long been the quintessential detective: the standard by which all others are judged.

To fully appreciate Holmes's genius, however, we must understand something of the world in which he lived and plied his trade: the bustling, grimy, fog-benighted London of the late Victorian era, which plays a starring role in many of the detective's adventures. In those days it was a city just emerged from an industrial revolution that had transformed it almost beyond recognition. From just 850,000 citizens in 1810, its population had exploded to more than six million by the turn of the twentieth century, turning London into one of the world's most colorful and cosmopolitan cities, teeming with immigrants newly arrived from Scotland, famine-plagued Ireland, Asia, Africa, continental Europe, and the Americas. It was the world's largest city and the capital of an empire which controlled the destinies of four hundred million subjects. As it grew eightfold in physical size in less than a century, sprouting suburbs many miles distant from the banks of the Thames, the original City of London and its ancient walls became merely the core of a sprawling, imposing metropolis. "One may go east or north or south or west" from the city center, wrote an overwhelmed American visitor in 1895, "and almost despair of ever reaching the rim."

At first, the police couldn't keep up. Extreme poverty in overcrowded slums had bred a vast criminal underclass dependent on petty thievery just to survive. By 1870 nearly a million Londoners were crowded into tenements along the mean streets of the East End, and those who couldn't find low-paying day labor at the docks, employment at one of the city's many sweat-shops, or some other form of subsistence income were often forced to choose between starvation and a life of crime. Scotland Yard, the police force whose jurisdiction was London's new urban sprawl, had been only instituted in 1829 and took fifty years or so to prove its effectiveness.

By the turn of the century, Scotland Yard had reduced crime in the city markedly, but forensic science was very much in its infancy, dedicated criminal investigators were a relatively new innovation, and Sherlock Holmes's opinion of them as well-meaning but ineffective was embraced with enthusiasm by Conan Doyle's readership. London was an optimistic city emerging from a troubled period in its history, and it needed brilliant, modern, scientifically minded do-gooders like Sherlock Holmes to strike at the still-beating heart of its criminal underworld. He was, in a way, the city's first superhero.

PART I.

DETECTIVE
SKILLS

How to Use Analytical Reasoning

From a drop of water, a logician could infer the possibility of an Atlantic or a Niagara without having seen or heard of one or the other. So all life is a great chain, the nature of which is known whenever we are shown a single link of it.

—from "The Book of Life," a monograph by Sherlock Holmes

he mere fact that you are holding this book allows one to make a number of elementary deductions concerning your disposition: that you nurture an interest in criminals and criminality; that you are at least passingly learned in the literary arts; and, like so many others, that you wish to cast a little light upon (and even emulate) Holmes's almost preternatural genius for reasoning backward from the thinnest of observed effects to uncannily accurate causes. His celebrated technique is called *analytical reasoning*, and when paired with a wide-ranging knowledge of forensics, the results can be striking. This is how you may employ it for yourself.

1. Become a masterful observer of minutiae. When presented with a mystery, minutiae are the small facts upon which large inferences often depend. For instance, in *The Sign of the Four*, Watson challenges Holmes's assertion that "it is difficult for a man to have any object in daily use without leaving the impress of his individuality upon it" by handing Holmes a watch that had recently come into Watson's possession. Putting Holmes's deductive abilities to the test, Watson asks him to describe "the character . . . of its late owner." Holmes begins by examining the object thoroughly, making the following observations:

- The watch is made of gold and was expensive when purchased.
- It is at least fifty years old.
- The initials *H.W.* are monogrammed on the back.
- There are four sets of numbers scratched on the inside of the watch case, a common mark of contemporary pawnbrokers.
- The watch is covered with scratches and dents.
- Especially deep scratches surround the keyhole used to wind the watch.

2. Develop a set of possible causes for the facts you have observed. For example, the *H.W.* monogram could mean that the watch had belonged either to some relative of

Dr. Watson's or to some unrelated person whose surname also happened to start with *W*. The scratches and dents could be explained by a careless owner who kept the watch in a pocket with keys and coins, wore it into battle, or allowed some animal to chew it. The scratches around the keyhole indicate a lack of hand-eye coordination when attempting to wind the watch, caused perhaps by some malady of the brain, blindness, or drunkenness or a habit of winding the watch while riding in carriages on poorly sealed roads.

3. Eliminate the least likely causes. Resist the urge to guess—"it is a shocking habit destructive to the logical faculty," counsels Holmes—and instead use Occam's Razor, a principle asserting that the simplest explanations are most often correct. In doing so, we may abandon the hypotheses that the watch's former owner was unrelated to Dr. Watson, brought the watch into battle, or was blind. This method is not *always* guaranteed to produce accurate results—even Holmes will admit that his spectacular inferences are only "the balance of probability"—but with a bit of luck and intuition, your analyses will prove correct more often than not. Though mere mortals may find themselves unequal to Holmes's special abilities in this regard, this is what the great detective infers from his few observations:

- From the timepiece's worn condition, he deduces that anyone "who treats a fifty-guinea watch so cavalierly must be a careless man. Neither is it a very far-fetched inference that a man who inherits one article of such value is pretty well provided for in other respects."
- The inscription *H.W.* most likely suggests Watson's own name. Holmes reasons that, given that the watch

is fifty years old, it probably belonged to Watson's father, and because it is tradition for such items of jewelry to descend to the eldest son, it was therefore inherited by Watson's older brother.

- The pawnbroker's marks suggest the owner was often low on funds, but that after having repeatedly pawned the watch, a "burst of prosperity" allowed him to regain it on at least three occasions.

- The scratches around the keyhole are obviously marks where the key missed its intended target. "What sober man's key could have scored those grooves?" Holmes posits.

4. Synthesize your inferences into a story that explains the facts. Gathering all his deductions, Holmes weaves the following narrative: Watson's eldest brother "was a man of untidy habits—very untidy and careless. He was left with good prospects, but he threw away his chances, lived for some time in poverty with occasional short intervals of prosperity, and finally, taking to drink, he died." Gobsmacked, Watson concedes that Holmes's analyses are "absolutely correct in every particular." Was Holmes lucky? In some respects, he was—but the well-applied principles of analytical reasoning helped steer him toward the truth.

Sherlock Holmes, Scientist

He would hardly reply to my questions, and busied himself all evening in an abstruse chemical analysis which involved much heating of retorts and distilling of vapors, ending at last in a smell which fairly drove me out of the apartment.

—Dr. Watson, *The Sign of the Four*

herlock Holmes was a student of science who became a master of detection. When Watson first encounters him in *A Study in Scarlet*, Holmes is performing an experiment in a chemical laboratory, and his first words, appropriately enough, are "I've found it! I've found it!" Running toward Watson with a test-tube in his hand, the young detective cries, "I have found a re-agent which is precipitated by hemoglobin, and by nothing else." His studies, a mutual friend explains, are eccentric: though Holmes is "an enthusiast in some branches of science" and "a first-class chemist," he has never taken "any systematic medical classes." What his school colleagues didn't know is that Holmes was honing the unique skills he would need to become one of the world's first forensic scientists, or, in his own words, "filling in my too abundant leisure time by studying all those branches of science which might make me more efficient."

By bringing the scientific method to bear on his work as a detective, Holmes fashioned himself into a most effective criminal investigator.

Among the natural sciences, chemistry was Holmes's overriding passion. He spent much of his free time performing chemical experiments in the Baker Street apartments, and during his mysterious three-year hiatus following his faked death in "The Final Problem," he spent several months in France researching "coal-tar derivatives." (Holmes scholar Joseph Dence explains that was "then one of the most fertile" areas of chemical study.) Though chemistry in the Victorian era lacked many of the sophisticated instruments and methodologies it enjoys today, modern chemists now consider Holmes's period a golden age of discovery; new elements were being identified and added to the periodic table almost yearly, and so many useful, naturally occurring substances were coming to light that much of chemists' time was spent simply identifying them and cataloguing their properties.

Geology was an extremely popular field of study in Holmes's day. Debate raged over the age of the Earth (which wouldn't be accurately determined until the middle of the twentieth century), with estimates ranging from 100,000 to several billion years old. Geologists generally divided into two camps: the catastrophists, who believed the Earth was relatively young and had been shaped by a series of abrupt cataclysmic events (like the Biblical flood), and uniformitarianists, who thought the Earth was ancient and had evolved gradually over a long period (which meshed with Darwin's theories). Sherlock Holmes, who "would acquire no knowledge which did not bear upon his object," had no opinion on the matter. Watson assessed his knowledge of geology thusly: "Practical, but limited. Tells at a glance different soils from each other. After walks has shown me splashes upon his trousers, and told me by their color and consistence in what part of London he had received them." Ever the pragmatist, the only mysteries Holmes could be bothered with were those that pertained to murder, thieving, and other forms of human wickedness.

Botany was another of his specialties, particularly when it came to "belladonna, opium, and poisons." He "knows nothing of practical gardening," Watson reports, which is consistent with Holmes's interests; he was much more likely to come across a murder victim killed by deadly nightshade than by anything found growing in a garden plot. Professional botanists of Holmes's day inhabited a comparatively mature field of study relative to chemistry or physics, disciplines still in their adolescence. Promising students of the day were discouraged against studying botany, about which, it was thought, almost everything had already been discovered.

Watson also notes Holmes's "accurate but unsystematic" knowledge of anatomy—we may assume he was self-taught, which explains reports of a young Holmes "beating the subjects in the dissecting-rooms with a stick . . . to verify how far bruises may be produced after death." He knew nothing of astronomy, not even the composition of the solar system, to which an astonished Watson replies that "any civilized human being in this nineteenth century" should be at least glancingly familiar. As for this and the rest of the sciences with which the great detective was unashamedly unfamiliar, Holmes says that "a man should keep his little brain-attic stocked with all the furniture that he is likely to use"—and little else.

How to Question a Suspect

"Be frank with me, and we may do some good. Play tricks with me, and I'll crush you."
—Sherlock Holmes, "The Abbey Grange"

he primary goal when questioning a suspect is not to glean new information about the crime—the nature and events of which an astute detective has already reconstructed—but to determine whether or not the suspect being questioned is telling the truth. To that end, what the suspect says is equally if not less important than the manner in which he expresses it. As Holmes himself writes, "a twitch of a muscle or glance of an eye" allows the expertly trained detective "to fathom a man's inmost thoughts," making deceit "an impossibility."

- **Do your homework.** Arm yourself with as much knowledge about the crime and the suspect as possible prior to the

"WHAT THE SUSPECT SAYS IS EQUALLY IF NOT LESS IMPOR-
TANT THAN THE MANNER IN WHICH HE EXPRESSES IT."

interview. If you have the facts at your command, you stand a much better chance of judging truth from deception.

• **Begin with a few "control" questions.** These can be simple biographical questions about the subject meant to establish a rapport and put them at ease or questions about the case to which you already know the answers, designed to establish the general truthfulness of the suspect. Observe the suspect's behavior while answering control questions and closely monitor changes in behavior during subsequent questioning.

• **Avoid yes-or-no questions.** Ask questions that elicit narrative answers; the more details a suspect is forced to provide, the more likely that a lie will fail to square with known facts or that the suspect will contradict himself. In *The Valley of Fear*, Holmes is certain two suspects have woven "a great, big, thumping, obtrusive, uncompromising lie" because the details of their stories don't jibe with his knowledge about the circumstances of the crime: *"How do I know that they are lying? Because it is a clumsy fabrication which simply could not be true. Consider! According to the story given to us, the assassin had less than a minute after the murder had been committed to take that ring, which was under another ring, from the dead man's finger, to* *replace the other ring . . . I say that this was obviously impossible."*

• **Look for nonverbal cues.** Even if a suspect is a master of deception—such as Holmes's archenemy Professor Moriarty, whose "soft, precise fashion of speech leaves a conviction of sincerity"—his body language may still give him away. There are subtle, instinctual gestures one makes when lying that are beyond conscious control and that the trained eye can recognize. Avoiding eye contact, for instance, signals discomfort. Looking up and tilting one's head to the right while answering may signify deceit, while looking down indicates sincerity and a genuine attempt to recall information. Open hands suggest honesty, while closed or fidgeting hands can signal the opposite. Crossing the arms is a sign of uneasiness, while rubbing the chin has been interpreted to mean that a suspect doesn't believe what he is hearing. Contemporary psychologists such as Paul Ekman have written at length about the validity of these various cues.

• **Act as though you know the truth—even if you don't.** During an interrogation, knowledge is power, and if a suspect believes you already know much of the truth, she is more likely to be forthcoming. In "The Mazarin Stone," Holmes ingeniously tricks the cunning Count Sylvius into admitting he knows the location of the missing stone by bluffing that he *already* knows and priming the Count for information about its location. By maintaining that he'll never tell, the Count confesses his guilt.

• **Try bargaining.** If you need to extract information from a recalcitrant suspect or witness, make admitting the truth seem like the lesser of two evils. Once Holmes has elicited a confession from the Count, he makes an offer the Count cannot refuse: "We want the stone. Give that up, and so far as I am concerned you can go free." Otherwise, Holmes threatens, the Count will be "locked up for twenty years."

How to Decode Ciphers

"I am fairly familiar with all forms of secret writings, and am myself the author of a trifling monograph upon the subject, in which I analyze one hundred and sixty separate ciphers."

—Sherlock Holmes, "The Adventure of the Dancing Men"

riting in cipher, also known as cryptography, is the art of composing messages meant to be incomprehensible to anyone save the intended recipient, who (one would hope) possesses its key. For the interceptor of a ciphered message, the first problem is to determine what type of cipher has been used. This is a matter of trial, error, and educated guesswork, for decryption is often more art than science. But as Holmes points out in his "Dancing Men" case, there are "rules which guide us in all forms of secret writing," and if one is familiar with them, it is possible that any cipher may be discovered and its message revealed. To that end, we will examine a few of the types of ciphers that Holmes unravels during the course of his career.

THE SUBSTITUTION CIPHER

This is the type of cipher Holmes famously decrypts in "The Dancing Men," which replaces letters in a message with what seems at first like childish nonsense but which Holmes quickly deduces to be symbols that correspond to letters in the English alphabet. Using a slightly modified "dancing-man" alphabet, we've encrypted a new message:

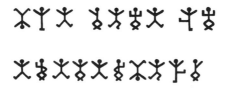

Having no knowledge of the substitution alphabet used to create it, how can this gibberish be made sense of without endless and taxing guesswork? Thusly:

1. Using frequency analysis, the decipherer's first business is to classify the letters in the message according to their rate of recurrence in the alphabet. This too is Holmes's first step: "As you are aware, *e* is the most common letter in the English alphabet," he explains, "and it predominates to so marked an extent that even in a short sentence one would expect to find it most often." Of the nineteen letters in the encrypted message above, five are " ✗ ," and so we may assume with reasonable assurance that " ✗ " is an encrypted substitute for the letter *e*.

2. Single letters occurring in isolation must be *a*, *I*, or in rare cases *o*. Groupings of two letters occurring together are *ee*, *oo*, *ff*, and *ss*. Because there are none of either sort in the encrypted message, continue to the next step.

3. The most common words of two letters, roughly arranged in order of their frequency, are *of*, *to*, *in*, *it*, *is*, *be*, *he*, *by*, *or*, *as*, *at*, *an*, and *so*. At this juncture we lack adequate information regarding " ⳑ ⳡ ," the only two-letter word in the sequence. Return to it when you know more.

4. Notice that " ⚹⑂⚹ ," the first encrypted word, contains one previously decoded letter, " ⚹ ," which was reasoned to be a substitute for *e*. Because the most common of three-letter words is *the*, and the final letter of the first word in our sequence is *e*, we may infer that " ⚹⑂⚹ " stands for *the*. This reveals two further letters of the substitution alphabet: " ⚹ ," a substitute for *t*, and " ⑂ ," a substitute for *h*. We may also replace the " ⚹ " in the final word with *t*.

5. The partially decoded message now reads: "The ⚹ ⚹ ⚹ e ⑂ ⚹ e ⚹ e ⚹ e ⚹ t ⚹ ⑂ ⚹ . " Since alphabetical frequency analysis is less helpful with words in excess of three or four letters, turn instead to contextual and grammatical clues. Being that this is a book about Sherlock Holmes, you might apply a bit of contextual frequency analysis and speculate that the final word in the sequence is the word most famously associated with Holmes himself: *elementary*.

6. With this deduction, one further letter in the sequence is solved: " ⚹ ," which is clearly a substitution for *a*. With much of the message decoded, it doesn't require a great effort of the mind to convert the message into its deciphered form: "The case is elementary!"

THE VALLEY OF FEAR CIPHER

In this adventure, Holmes must decrypt a substitution cipher of a different sort. He has in his possession a coded message from a confederate of the nefarious Professor Moriarty, which reads:

534 C2 13 127 36 31 4 17 21 41

DOUGLAS 109 293 5 37 BIRLSTONE

26 BIRLSTONE 9 47 171

Confounded at first, Holmes says, "It is clearly a reference to the words in a page of some book. Until I am told which page and which book I am powerless." Being who he is, however, the detective soon deduces that the book must be a large one—the first number refers to page 534—and that C2 refers not to the second chapter, but the second column on the aforementioned page. Further, all the numbers after the page and column designations refer to words in that second column, which, if they go as high as 293, indicate a long column indeed.

That narrows the books to which the ciphered message could be referring. Watson suggests it might be the Bible, though Holmes ridicules this suggestion, saying, "I could hardly name any volume which would be less likely to lie at the elbow of one of

Moriarty's associates"—and besides, there are so many editions of the Bible that the pagination from one to another could hardly be expected to match. Instead, Holmes hits upon a large, multi-columned book of standardized formatting that was common in households: *Whitaker's Almanac*. The words "Douglas" and "Birlstone" were names that could not both be expected to appear on a random page of the printed almanac, so were written out by the message's encoder.

When Holmes and Watson find the second column of the 534th page of the almanac, the message is easily decipherable: "There is danger – may – come – very – soon – one. 'Douglas' – 'rich – country – now – at – Birlstone – House – Birlstone – confidence – is – pressing." "The purport is perfectly clear," Holmes explains to Watson. "Some deviltry is intended against one Douglas, whoever he may be, residing as stated, a rich country gentleman. He is sure – 'confidence' was as near as he could get to 'confident' – that it is pressing. There is our result – and a very workmanlike little bit of analysis it was!"

How to Analyze Footprints

"There is no branch of detective science which is so important and so much neglected as the art of tracing footsteps."

—Sherlock Holmes, *A Study in Scarlet*

 criminal may wear gloves to avoid leaving fingerprints at a crime scene, but, lacking wings, he cannot avoid walking through it. To the trained eye, footprints can be as distinctive as fingerprints: Holmes, the author of a monograph on the subject, could from examining a single set of tracks describe the probable height, weight, sex, economic status, and even the emotional disposition of the poor soul who left them, if not their owner's very name. It follows that footprints and tracks are of paramount importance when investigating a crime scene.

• **Search for footprints.** Because one can only analyze footprints if there are footprints to be discovered, wet weather is a detective's best friend. Mud and clay are ideal media in which to discover tracks of all kinds, not simply because they take foot impressions well but because they cling to one's shoes, creating footprints where none may otherwise be found. Begin your search in any nearby soft-soiled garden beds or muddy lanes, then move toward the scene of the crime in a circular pattern to determine whether any prints have been tracked onto it.

• **Follow the tracks.** If they are fresh, your suspect may still be close at hand. Follow them—preferably with a pistol or police escort—and you just might find your perpetrator. Holmes and Watson follow a set of bicycle tracks over a muddy moor in "The Solitary Cyclist"—they know the direction the bike was traveling because the rear tire-track is a bit deeper—and come upon the cyclist himself, dead.

• **Make a cast.** Prior to commencing any serious analysis, it is vital to preserve a copy of the footprints in case anything should happen to them in the course of your investigation. Cast-making is an art unto itself—one with which Holmes, who has written about "the uses of plaster of Paris as a preserver of impresses," is intimately familiar. Generally speaking, wet plaster is poured into the foot impression, hardened, and removed, providing a permanent record of the print (or wheel mark, hoof print, or paw print).

• **Reconstruct the crime.** There is much that footprints can reveal about the manner in which a crime was committed. Different sets of prints point to the number of perpetrators involved, whereas a great number of the same prints could mean the crime was premeditated; that the criminal spent considerable time at the scene, either lying in wait for the victim or plotting an escape after the deed was done. If there are but a few prints, however, you can be sure the perpetrator did not linger long, suggesting it may have been a crime of impulse or passion.

• **Measure the length of the foot and stride.** In *A Study in Scarlet*, Holmes judges a suspect to be quite tall by measuring the unusual distance between the left and right footprints, that is, the stride. Height can be corroborated by measuring the length of the foot impression: Generally, the foot composes about fifteen percent of an individual's height. Dividing the length of the bare foot by 0.15 gives a rough estimate of its owner's stature. (For shoe impressions, which add a bit of length, divide by 0.16.) What's more, the angle of the feet relative to each other can be significant: "That left foot of yours with its inward twist is all over the place," Holmes tells Inspector Lestrade while investigating a crime scene in "The Boscombe Valley Mystery."

• **Note the style and wear pattern of the shoe.** A familiarity with sole impressions left by different types of shoes is helpful. In the same case mentioned above, Holmes was also able to ascertain that a suspect was fashionably dressed, judging from "the small and elegant impression left by his boots." In much the same way, a terribly worn or out-of-fashion boot may indicate that a criminal is a pauper.

• **Examine the depth and completeness of the footprints.** Especially deep prints could mean a suspect was heavy or laden down with a burdensome object. The footprints of a running man will be incomplete, as Holmes observed in *The Hound of the Baskervilles*: What appeared to investigators to be the tracks of a man walking on tip-toes were actually, Holmes reasoned, made by a man "running for his life."

• **Match the footprints to a suspect's boots.** In "The

Adventure of the Beryl Coronet," Holmes ingeniously disguises himself as a tramp so that he may buy the cast-off shoes of a well-to-do suspect without arousing suspicion and is able to match them to footprints left at a crime scene.

BE AWARE

Footprints may be the most damning sort of track evidence, but they shouldn't be focused on to the exclusion of all else. Giant canine tracks play a crucial role in Holmes's solution to The Hound of the Baskervilles; *cow and bicycle tracks in "The Priory School"; carriage tracks in "The Greek Interpreter"; and horse tracks in "Silver Blaze."*

The Creatures of Sherlock Holmes's World

In mere size and strength it was a terrible creature which was lying stretched before us.
—The Hound of the Baskervilles

reatures in the Holmes canon are as likely to be used as murder weapons as they are as pets. Rarely docile and never cute—unless they're being tortured by cruel children in "The Copper Beeches," hurled through plate-glass windows in "The Lion's Mane," or poisoned to death in *A Study in Scarlet*—most of the animals that rate mention by Dr. Watson are of the stinging, teeth-gnashing, or poisonous variety. In Holmes's world, if a creature is capable of killing someone, it probably will.

• **The Hound of the Baskervilles** is easily the most famous, but perhaps the least deadly, of the canon's creatures. At the risk of spoiling the mystery for any who haven't read it, the "luminous, ghastly and spectral" canine who stalks the moors of West Country England and "fills the air with its howling" turns out not to be a supernatural hell-hound at all. When it leaps menacingly out of the darkness at Holmes and Watson late in the story—"never in the delirious dream of a disordered brain could anything more savage, more appalling, more hellish be conceived," writes a shaken Watson— Holmes empties his revolver into it, whereupon the creature lets out a "hideous howl" and collapses dead to the ground, demonstrably mortal. The terrible mouth from which fire had seemed to burst, the eyes that "glowed with a smolder-

ing glare" and the muzzle that had been "outlined in flickering flame" drip with a liquid preparation of luminescent phosphorous, applied by the dog's scheming owner. The laws of nature, it seems, remain firmly intact.

• "It is a **swamp adder**," cried Holmes, "the deadliest snake in India!" Used as a slithering murder weapon in "The Speckled Band," this deadly reptile is wielded by a ruthless stepfather upon his daughters, whose proposed marriages threaten to bankrupt him. He's trained the snake to descend a rope bell-pull in the intended victim's bedroom at the sounding of a whistle, bite the sleeper—its undetectable venom kills almost instantly—then escape by climbing the rope again, so that the cause of death remains a mystery. According to skeptical herpetologists, however, there is no such snake in India, and even if there were, snakes are deaf and so cannot respond to whistles; moreover they are physically incapable of climbing ropes.

• "The Lion's Mane" mystery is named for the culprit whom Holmes deduces to be the killer in this case: an enormous *Cyanea capillata*, also known as the **Lion's mane jellyfish**. The largest known jellyfish in the world, its tentacles can spread more than one hundred feet and administer a sting that Holmes rightly calls "as dangerous to life as, and far more painful than, the bite of a cobra." Found in cold waters— like those lapping the Sussex beach where the victim is found, covered in mysterious red welts— the *Cyanea* is one of the oldest and most primitive life forms on Earth. Though it lacks a heart, a brain, and even a central nervous system, this jellyfish's terrible tentacles contain more than enough toxins to paralyze a human victim's muscles, including, in deadly cases, the heart and lungs.

• **A killer circus lion** figures prominently in the case of "The Veiled Lodger," in which a disfigured former lion trainer confesses a crime of passion to Holmes. Her late husband, a cruel and vicious lion tamer, was not killed in the lion attack that destroyed her face, as she has always claimed. The real killer was her former lover, who did in her husband with

a nail-spiked club meant to simulate the wounds an angry lion might inflict. Upon seeing its tamer murdered, however, the lion went mad and attacked the woman—but to her dismay, spared her life. "When I came to myself and saw myself in the mirror," she explains, "I cursed that lion – *oh, how I cursed him!* – not because he had torn away my beauty but because he had not torn away my life."

• **Langur monkeys** are central to the mystery of "The Creeping Man," in which an aging, brilliant professor begins acting strangely shortly before his wedding to a younger woman. His bizarre symptoms include a "sinister" change in his character, "thick and horny" knuckles, a new propensity to be attacked by his faithful old dog, and an incident in which he climbs the creeper vines growing up the walls of his house. All of which were preceded by a mysterious visit to Prague, during which Holmes suspects the professor became addicted to some strange drug. After observing his animalistic behavior for themselves—his "dignified figure crouching frog-like on the ground" and climbing vines "with incredible agility"—Holmes and Watson find a letter from a quack doctor in Prague, revealing that the professor has been prescribed an aphrodisiac made from the blood of the black-faced langur. "Langur is, of course, a crawler and a climber," the letter warns. In his misguided quest to please a much-younger bride, it seems, a highly evolved man has turned himself into an animal. "When one tries to rise above Nature," Holmes pontificates, "one is liable to fall below it."

How to Locate a Secret Chamber

An amazing thing happened. A door suddenly flew
open out of what appeared to be solid wall at the
end of the corridor, and a little, wizened man darted
out of it, like a rabbit out of its burrow.
—"The Norwood Builder"

any old houses possess secret chambers for the con-
cealment of valuables, compromising deeds, or wanted
persons, and what ancient castle, monastery, or hall has
not its traditional subterranean passage? But mere certainty that a
secret passage or gloomy hiding-hole lurks behind the wainscot-
ing makes them no easier to bear out: Their entranceways are
often well disguised; their architects master craftsmen. Sherlock
Holmes discovered at least three such chambers in his storied
career, none of which were hidden in the same way. Commence
your search with the most obvious possibilities, keeping in mind

that, as Holmes himself has demonstrated, the most successful techniques are sometimes the least conventional.

• **Search behind moveable objects.** Many a secret door has been hidden behind a bookcase, an armoire, or a full-length mirror. Proceed systematically through the house, checking behind all such objects.

• **Take up the rugs.** Wobbly or loose floor boards may be a door in disguise.

• **Knock on the walls.** A hollow-sounding return is a tell-tale sign of a hidden cavity. If no door is evident, it may be necessary to cut an exploratory hole through the wall.

• **Measure the dimensions of the house.** In an attempt to determine whether a fabulous store of treasure might be hidden in a secret compartment inside his house, *The Sign of the Four*'s scheming Bartholomew Sholto "worked out all the cubic space of the house, and made measurements everywhere, so that not one inch should be unaccounted for." Adding together the height of all the separate rooms, he discovered that there were a few cubic feet missing. He "knocked a hole, therefore, in the plaster ceiling of the high-

est room, and there, sure enough, he came upon another little garret above it, which had been sealed up and was known
to no one. In the centre stood the treasure-chest, resting
upon two rafters."

• **Probe the interior of chimney stacks** with a strong
flashlight. Be aware that certain chimneys are split into tree-
like arrangements, and it's not unheard of for one branching
offshoot or another to have been cunningly bricked up and
divided from the primary chimney, wherein a person might
hide, free from flame, smoke, or discovery by bungling
detectives.

• **Identify uneven furrows in the grass.** Occasionally, a
chamber or passageway may be located on the grounds of an
old house, its entrance hidden beneath the sod. Unusual
depressions in the soil may indicate a chamber beneath;
locate perceptibly uneven patches and drive a stake into them
to a depth of at least a meter. If the stake should encounter
something immoveable, dig.

• **Smoke out your prey.** If you've reason to suspect that a
living person is hiding in an unknown chamber, this technique—made famous by Holmes in "The Norwood

"MANY A SECRET DOOR HAS BEEN HIDDEN BEHIND A BOOK-
CASE, AN ARMOIRE, OR A FULL-LENGTH MIRROR."

Builder"—will flush him out without your needing to peek behind a single mirror or bookcase. Place a bale of dry straw on a fireproof surface in the middle of the house, making sure to keep it at a prudent remove from the walls. Hold a match to it, adding straw to the blaze until clouds of smoke billow through the rooms. Solicit a chorus of able-voiced assistants to shout *"FIRE!"* as loudly as possible. Before long, self-preservative instincts will surely drive the hidden party from his burrow. Douse the fire with a bucket of water and apprehend your suspect.

• **Wait.** Should you have the manpower to post a guard in each room, the least destructive option may simply be to wait. In due time the hidden scoundrel will reveal himself— and the secret room—or risk dying of hunger or thirst.

• **Pretend to give up the search.** Proceed from room to room announcing that the search has been a failure: *"Such a pity we failed to locate the secret chamber! Good-bye!"* Make loud clomping footsteps toward the door, slam it, then keep very quiet. With any luck, this clever bit of subterfuge will coax the hidden party into the open.

BE AWARE

If your quarry is hiding in an old London mansion, you may wish to check the home for a tiny cramped hideaway known as a priest-hole. Catholics were persecuted by law during the reigns of monarchs Elizabeth I and James I, and as such many British homes from the six- teenth century contain human-sized secret chambers built to secret away hunted clergymen. One of the best-known architects of such chambers was a Jesuit carpenter named Nicholas Owen, who was elected to sainthood for devoting twenty years of his life to the construction of priest-holes, a crime for which he was martyred on the rack in 1606. "With incompa- rable skill," writes an authority, "he knew how to conduct priests to a place of safety along subterranean passages, to hide them between walls and bury them in impenetrable recesses, and to entangle them in labyrinths and a thousand windings. But what was much more difficult of accom- plishment, he so disguised the entrances to these as to make them most unlike what they really were." Some of Owen's remarkable priest-holes may yet remain undiscovered.

How to Examine a Body at a Crime Scene

As he spoke, his nimble fingers were flying here, there, and everywhere, feeling, pressing, unbuttoning, examining, while his eyes wore the same far-away expression which I have already remarked upon. So swiftly was the examination made, that one would hardly have guessed the minuteness with which it was conducted. Finally, he sniffed the dead man's lips, and then glanced at the soles of his patent leather boots.

—*A Study in Scarlet*

 consulting detective rarely enjoys the advantage of being the first to arrive at a crime scene, but should you turn up and find the body yet unexamined—or examined by detectives of lesser intellects, if the entire scene hasn't already been washed clear of evidence by some oafish constable—heed Sherlock Holmes's advice. Unusual murders that most people find perplexing, he explains in *A Study in Scarlet*, are the easiest for astute detectives to solve: "Strange details, far from making the case more difficult, [have] the effect of making it less so." What follows is a system for making observations that will leave no unusual detail undiscovered.

- **Make sure the victim is actually dead.** Certain poisons derived from exotic plants and animals can induce a death-like state in their victims; there are documented cases of such persons being buried or cremated while still alive. Holmes and Watson narrowly avoid such a tragedy in "The Disappearance of Lady Frances Carfax," when they discover the Lady Carfax, chloroformed and profoundly unconscious, inside a nailed-shut coffin. For the sake of thoroughness, hold a mirror before the victim's nostrils and press two fingers against the neck, or, as Holmes did in *Scarlet*, sniff the body's lips so that you might detect a whiff of some narcotizing toxin. Should you discover that the victim is not quite dead, quickly attempt to coax out a statement. (Questions such as "Who attempted to murder you?" leap to mind.)

- **Determine the cause of death.** Look for obvious wounds such as gunshots, bludgeon strikes, bruises, or strangulation marks. Also check for secondary wounds like bloodied knuckles, which may suggest a struggle, or defensive wounds like gunshots on the hands or upper arms. Do your observations square with the accounts of witnesses?

• **Examine the clothing.** Tears on clothing may indicate a struggle. Bunched clothing could mean the body was dragged away from the true murder scene.

• **Look for bloodstains.** If a large amount of blood is present, look for drag marks, which could mean that the body had been moved. Also, ensure that bloodstains correspond to a wound on the victim; in *A Study in Scarlet*, Holmes determines that blood spattered on a woundless corpse "belongs to a second individual—presumably the murderer."

• **Check for missing valuables.** Is the victim still in possession of a billfold and jewelry? Is he clutching anything in his hands? Examine the wrist and fingers for tan lines, which could indicate a purloined ring or wristwatch (thus suggesting robbery as the killer's possible motive). If no valuables can be found on the body, check the surrounding area; a ring found near the victim in *A Study in Scarlet* is the key that allows Holmes to find the murderer.

• **Determine the approximate time of death.** A truly detailed analysis of time of death must be performed by a specialist, but a few quick observations by an astute detective can be useful nevertheless. When Holmes discovers a body in the famous secret chamber of "The Musgrave Ritual," he quickly determines that it has been dead "for some days" by

noting its "distorted liver-colored countenance" and the "stagnant blood" pooling in its face. In *A Study in Scarlet*, Holmes deduces that the victim has been expired "for some time, for his limbs were rigid and cold." The stiffening phenomenon Holmes observes is known as *rigor mortis*, and it occurs between three and seventy-two hours after death.

• **If the victim is unknown, attempt to deduce the person's identity.** Though an unclaimed body may lack identification, there are numerous ways to discover its identity. Holmes himself wrote a monograph on the subject of identifying a victim's profession by "the form of the hand," declaring that the hands of "slaters, sailors, corkcutters, compositors, weavers, and diamond-polishers," to name just a few, were easily distinguishable from one another. The victim's clothes and the neighborhood in which the body is discovered are other clues.

How to Analyze Bullet Evidence

Holmes held it out to me. "A soft revolver bullet, as you perceive, Watson. There's genius in that, for who would expect to find such a thing fired from an air-gun?"

—"The Adventure of the Empty House"

ust as a criminal's footprints and fingerprints become silent witnesses against him in the hands of a capable detective, so too does the evidence left behind by a criminal's gun. Though Sherlock Holmes rarely carried one, he was familiar with firearms of all types, the bullets they required, and the traces they made when discharged. To analyze a crime scene in which a firearm was employed, a detective need not be an expert in ballistics; rather, a few elementary techniques can do much to reconstruct the crime and aid in tracking the criminal.

- **Mark the location of any shell casings.** These will reveal several pieces of the puzzle, including the number of shots fired and the general location of the shooter. In the "Dancing Men" mystery, Holmes casts doubt upon the suspected murder-suicide of a couple in their home when he discovers a shell casing in a trampled flowerbed just outside a nearby window, which implies a third shooter.

- **Match shell casings to bullet holes.** A bullet hole found in the windowsill—in addition to one each in husband and wife—further confirms the presence of a third shooter in "The Dancing Men." Because the husband's pistol (the only firearm at the crime scene) has two chambers empty, Holmes reasons that rather than the wife shooting her husband and then herself, a third party shot through the window at the husband, who returned fire (hence the bullet hole in the windowsill) whereupon the wife, in despair, turned her husband's gun upon herself. Without accounting for every shot fired by matching shell casings to bullet holes, this deduction would not have been possible.

• **Look for gunpowder residue.** In "The Reigate Squires," Holmes concludes that a victim was shot from more than four yards away because he could find "no powder-blackening on the clothes." Persons fired upon at close range often show evidence of stippled burn marks on the face or clothing, made by the still-ignited gunpowder ejected from a gun's barrel when a bullet is fired.

• **Match the bullets to a gun.** The murder weapon is usually one of the detective's strongest pieces of evidence. A cursory visual inspection will reveal the characteristic markings that firearms leave on intact bullets, which differ greatly from model to model and subtly between differing guns of the same model type. In "The Problem of Thor Bridge," Holmes suspects that police have misinterpreted bullet evidence: When a revolver of the model type that killed a woman is found in her maid's wardrobe, police assume that the maid is

"FAMILIARIZE YOURSELF WITH ALL MANNER OF FIREARMS
AND BULLET CASINGS."

her employer's killer. But Holmes proves otherwise, demonstrating that the woman managed to shoot herself but planted a gun of the same type in the maid's wardrobe while dropping the real murder weapon into a river after the fatal shot was fired. (An ingeniously cruel final act if ever there was one: The woman fired the fatal shot by tying the trigger to a long rope wound around a rock, then pointed the gun at herself while dropping the rock into a river.) Therefore, as damning as ballistics evidence can seem, it should never be the only factor upon which your case rests.

Victorian Firearms

I have always held, too, that pistol practice should be distinctly an open-air pastime; and when Holmes, in one of his queer humors, would sit in an arm-chair with his hair-trigger and a hundred Boxer cartridges, and proceed to adorn the opposite wall with a patri-otic V. R. done in bullet-pocks, I felt strongly that neither the atmosphere nor the appearance of our room was improved by it.

—Dr. Watson, "The Musgrave Ritual"

here were nearly a quarter million privately owned guns across England in Holmes's day, and few laws to restrict their use. The toothless 1903 Pistols Act was little more than a token gesture, mandating easy-to-obtain licenses for concealed handguns and making it illegal to sell firearms to anyone demonstrably "drunken or insane." Despite the ubiquity of guns, however, the average number of crimes involving firearms in London at that time was just forty-five per year; compare that to more than three thousand by the turn of the next century.

Holmes and Watson each owned and occasionally carried handguns—Watson was a decorated veteran of Britain's Second Anglo-Afghan War, after all—though they weren't often put to use. Holmes dispatches the titular hound of the Baskervilles with a rare flourish of his revolver, and in "The Copper Beeches" Watson saves a man from another vicious dog with the quick action of his own pistol. Theirs was a culture that owned and admired firearms but, outside wartime, didn't use them much. Here are some of the guns that Holmes might've encountered on the street, or Watson on the field of battle.

• Scholars have argued that Watson and Holmes both owned **Webley revolvers**, various models of which were standard issue for the British armed forces from the 1880s

through the 1940s. The Webley was a "top-break" revolver, meaning it was loaded by unlocking a hinge that exposed the cartridge cylinder. Top-breaks are today nearly extinct, having been replaced by more common swing-out cylinder designs.

• **Pepperbox revolvers** were an early competitor to cartridge cylinder revolvers, notable for their signature cluster of rotating barrels—anywhere from four to thirty-two of them, depending on the model—giving the guns a stout look not unlike that of a pepper shaker. Although they found devoted fans in both Britain and the United States, pepperboxes were expensive to produce and never officially adopted by any of the major branches of either nation's armed services. Production had ceased by the end of the nineteenth century.

• **Martini-Henry rifles** were carried into colonial wars by British soldiers for some thirty years, beginning in 1871. Replacing the Snider-Enfield, the Henry was a breech-loading, lever-activated rifle with an unprecedented rate of fire. One of the rifle's first true tests came during the Anglo-Zulu War in 1879, about which the British general Lord Chelmsford famously said, "I am inclined to think that the first experience of the Martini-Henrys will be such a surprise to the Zulus that they will not be formidable after the first effort." Although that did not quite prove to be the case, the Martini-Henry did receive partial credit for a stunning British victory at Rorke's Drift, during which 139 British soldiers successfully defended against at least four thousand Zulu warriors.

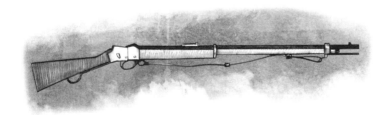

• The first modern machine gun was the **Maxim gun**, invented in 1884. Unlike the crank-operated Gatling and Gardner machine guns before it, the Maxim used the energy of its own recoil force to eject spent cartridges and load fresh ones; with it a gunner could achieve six hundred rounds of continuous fire per minute simply by holding down the trigger. It played a role in the swift colonization of Africa by British forces in the late nineteenth century, enabling just a few teams of Maxim-wielding soldiers to repel thousands of charging natives at a time. Perhaps the French-born writer Hilaire Belloc put it best when he penned this ditty: *Whatever happens, we have got / The Maxim gun, and they have not.*

• **Airguns** figure prominently in several Holmes stories, especially "The Empty House," in which the detective is hunted by vengeful snipers. Handling one after the case has been solved, Holmes calls it "an admirable and unique weapon . . . noiseless and of tremendous power." In use since the sixteenth century, these pneumatic pump-powered guns held several advantages. Not only could they be fired several times per minute, they also were much quieter and lacked the smoke and flash of traditional firearms, which could give away the shooter's firing position. Thus they were ideal for hunting (as well as sniping). They were expensive, however, and never attained the popularity of gunpowder-powered rifles.

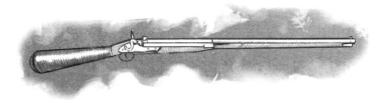

How to Crack a Safe

*With a glow of admiration I watched Holmes
unrolling his case of instruments and choosing his
tool with the calm, scientific accuracy of a surgeon
who performs a delicate operation. I knew that the
opening of safes was a particular hobby with him.*

—"The Adventure of Charles Augustus Milverton"

n theoretical terms, opening a safe is much like inter-
rogating a suspect: Both interrogator and safecracker
commence with the gentlest possible methods, but
when refined attempts are frustrated they must adopt successive-
ly more brutish techniques. In his "Charles Augustus Milverton"
adventure, Holmes drills into a notorious blackmailer's safe—not
the most delicate of techniques—which we must assume was
not secured by a combination lock, the code to which the great
detective surely would have been able to deduce. Though the
Holmes-era safecracking techniques outlined below may not

work on all types of modern safes (listening for points of contact would be pointless on a numerical-pad or digital combination lock, for instance), be assured that combination deduction, drilling, and the use of explosives will never go out of style amongst safecrackers.

LOCATE OR DEDUCE THE COMBINATION

With a little detective work, you may be able to open the safe without need of a drill, stethoscope, or dynamite stick.

1. Try all probable combinations. The professional should be intimately familiar not only with the type of safe he or she is attempting to open but with the person who owns it. Try combinations using the owner's birthday, address, telephone number, etc. Also, many safes are shipped bearing simple manufacturer-set combination codes that slothful owners have been known to leave unchanged; 000, 123, 321, and similar combinations should therefore be attempted.

2. Search for the combination. If you're unable to deduce the combination, have a look around. Astonishingly, many safe owners scribble their combinations on slips of paper and leave them nearby.

3. Pull on the handle. Before you start twiddling with the number wheel, try to open the safe. Bankers and businesspersons who use their safes regularly throughout the day sometimes close the safe door without locking it. Take advantage of their trusting nature and you might save yourself a considerable amount of trouble.

MANIPULATE THE LOCK

Should your detective skills prove unequal to deducing or discovering the combination, take heart: There remains a discreet way of gaining access to a safe without drills or explosives. With a finely tuned ear, a great deal of patience, and a morsel of luck you might manipulate the lock into revealing its combination.

1. Determine the points of contact. As you rotate the combination wheel 360 degrees, at some point you will hear a tiny, nearly inaudible *click*: This is where the bolt that prevents the safe from opening comes into contact with a small notch on the first disc. That subtle *click* represents one of the numbers needed to open the safe, though whether it is the first, second, or third remains a mystery. Take note of the number on the combination wheel when you hear the *click*.

2. Determine the number of discs in the lock. There are as many discs in a combination lock as there are numbers in the combination, up to a maximum of eight. To discover the number, "park" the combination wheel 180 degrees from the number of the first *click* you heard. Let the wheel rest there for a moment, then begin to turn it slowly to the right. Each time it passes the number at which it was parked, you will hear a *click* as the drive pin reengages with each combination disc. Count the number of *clicks* you hear, and you have determined the number of discs—and combination numbers—in the lock.

3. Listen for the contact clicks and record the results. Park the wheel at zero and turn it slowly to the left, listening for the tell-tale *click* of the contact point. Note the number where you hear it, then park the wheel a little farther to the left and continue repeating the process until you have traversed the entire circumference of the wheel. The numbers at which the *clicks* are loudest represent the numbers making up the combination.

4. Try every possible combination. Now that you know how many numbers are in the combination and roughly which numbers compose it, all that's left is to determine the order of the numbers. This is accomplished through simple trial and error. If there are three numbers in the combination and they are 3, 25, and 90, then the combination is either 3-25-90, 3-90-25, 25-3-90, 25-90-3, 90-3-25, or 90-25-3.

DRILL INTO THE SAFE

Should none of the combination possibilities gleaned from the above steps open the safe, it's probable your ears have failed you. Your only remaining option is to drill. There are many ways to drill into a safe, but we will address only the most straightforward method here.

1. Drill into the face of the lock. Whether your drill is hand powered, pneumatic, or electrical, it will take time, not to mention a very robust drill bit (diamond is ideal, though titanium will suffice) to penetrate the lock. Once you do, continue drilling until you reach the drive cam.

2. Use a punch rod to bend the drive cam. Using a punch rod narrow enough to fit into the hole you've just drilled but sturdy enough that it cannot easily be bent, force the drive cam out of the way. This may require a bit of monkeying, for you won't be able to see inside the hole you've drilled while it's filled with the punch rod you're manipulating. The longer the rod, the more leverage you will have and the simpler your task will be.

3. Open the safe. You'll know you've succeeded in bending the drive cam out of the way—thus making room for the bolt that stops the safe from opening to fall—when the door to the safe opens at last.

The Crimes of Sherlock Holmes

"We have shared the same room for some years, and it would be amusing if we ended by sharing the same cell. You know, Watson, I don't mind confessing to you that I have always had an idea that I would have made a highly efficient criminal."

—Sherlock Holmes, "The Adventure of Charles Augustus
Milverton"

olmes once famously said, "I had rather play tricks with the law of England than with my own conscience," and his ambivalence toward the strict letter of the law is borne out in practice throughout his adventures. Though his crimes may have been motivated by the best of intentions, crimes they remain, and as one critic put it, "Only a lightning calculator, thoroughly versed in the details of the penal code, could forthwith arrive at the length of time that Holmes, if indicted and tried, would have to serve for his multiple infractions." What follows is an examination of a few of his most egregious offenses.

• **Breaking and entering, theft, and being an accessory after the fact to murder.** Holmes's "Adventure of Charles

Augustus Milverton" is, despite strong competition, probably the detective's most felonious episode. In it, Holmes is hired by a young woman to rescue some damning letters from the clutches of the notorious blackmailer, Milverton, whom Holmes considers "the worst man in London." By disguising himself as a plumber and wooing Milverton's unsuspecting housemaid, Holmes discovers the location of the blackmail papers and hatches a plan to steal them. (In his single-minded pursuit of Milverton he even becomes engaged to the man's poor housemaid; certainly a crime of the heart if not of the law.) Donning black clothes and masks, Holmes and Watson use a "first-class, up-to-date burgling kit"—the mere possession of which is questionably legal—to break into Milverton's house in the dead of night. Holmes cracks the blackmailer's safe, in which the papers are kept, but before he and Watson can escape, a woman whom Holmes recognizes *also* breaks into the house and, much to their surprise, shoots Milverton dead. Holmes and Watson keep mum about the murderer's identity (making them accessories to the crime) and promptly destroy the contents of the blackmailer's safe before themselves fleeing the scene, thus indemnifying all of Milverton's other victims (and making themselves guilty of another crime, destruction of property). A jury might not convict Holmes and Watson for their various offenses against Milverton, but that does not make their actions any more legal!

• **Extortion** "Well, well," Holmes says at the conclusion of the "Three Gables" mystery, "I suppose I shall have to compound a felony as usual." When an elderly woman is chloroformed and a manuscript written by her deceased son stolen from her home, Holmes deduces the reason: The nefarious Isadora Klein, with whom the late writer had had an affair, wanted to stop the manuscript—a thinly veiled and damaging account of their relationship—from being published. Rather than presenting the matter to police, however, Holmes confronts Ms. Klein and demands that she buy the old woman a lavish trip around the world in return for his silence. She agrees, making Holmes an extortionist.

• **Fixing a horse race** Scholars have argued that Holmes may have placed an improper bet—and even skewed the odds in his own favor—in the sporting mystery "Silver Blaze." When a champion racehorse goes missing before a big race, its owner hires Holmes to find the beast. Holmes discovers that the horse has been hidden in plain sight—disguised with paint—but ever a fan of a well-timed dramatic revelations, he tells no one until the race is actually under way. Though still in disguise, the horse participates in the race, and when Holmes excuses himself at the sound of the bell—"I stand to win a little on this next race," he says— it's only natural to wonder if Holmes has capitalized on inside information (that the presumed-missing and therefore long-shot champion was actually running) by placing a bet on Silver Blaze. "There is no evidence," scholar Gavin Brend admits, but "knowing what Holmes knew about Silver Blaze, we should be very surprised if he had neglected this opportunity."

Sports columnist Red Smith is less kind to Holmes. He notes the detective's self-professed wealth in the 1891-set "Final Problem" adventure, and that just ten years later in "The Priory School" Holmes complains, "I am a poor man." Smith imagines a gambling addiction, suggesting that Holmes's wealth fluctuated wildly "because the bookies took everything he didn't have to lay out for happy dust," then accuses the detective of being "a horse player of degenerate principles who thought nothing of fixing a race, and when you bear in mind his first-hand knowledge of the use and effect of cocaine, he probably had his syringe in the veins of more than one thoroughbred." One thing is certain: Either Mr. Holmes is guilty of race fixing, or Mr. Smith is guilty of libel.

How to Analyze Fingerprints

"As he held the match nearer I saw that it was more than a stain. It was the well-marked print of a thumb."

—"The Adventure of the Norwood Builder"

 n the forensic study of fingerprints, Sherlock Holmes was well before his time. He recognized their importance as early as his 1894 "Norwood Builder" case, in which he proves that Scotland Yard's investigators have been duped by a print falsely planted to incriminate an innocent person. (In reality, Scotland Yard didn't establish its Fingerprint Branch until 1901, even though the science of fingerprinting had existed for some twenty years.) Despite great leaps forward in forensic science during the ensuing century, there is still little evidence more damning than a fingerprint. This is due to the simple fact that no two fingerprints are alike, and the properties of one's digital skin furrows are unchanging. When prints are clear and visually contrasted from the surface upon which they sit, it is a relatively simple task to identify matching finger impressions or distinguish between dissimilar ones—though a first-rate magnifying glass helps immensely.

1. Identify the quality of prints at the crime scene. If every criminal impressed his thumb into a pool of wax before fleeing the scene of his crime, identification would be a simple affair. Regrettably, such is not the custom, and the quality of prints a detective will encounter at a crime scene— if indeed any are found at all—vary greatly. They fall into three categories:

a. Patent prints occur when a foreign substance on the skin of a finger, such as blood or ink, comes into contact with a smooth surface. Such prints are usually visible to the naked eye.

b. Plastic prints result when a digit is pressed into a soft, malleable surface such as wax, chocolate, or wet paint. Easily observable, plastic prints are ideal.

c. Latent prints are transferred onto objects by oils or perspiration naturally present on the fingers and tend to leave behind a distinct but invisible impression. Physical, chemical, and electronic enhancement techniques may be required to view such prints.

2. Identify the pattern of the prints. The inner part of the hand is traversed in all directions by innumerable ridges of varying lengths that, though seemingly complex, can be classified with great accuracy. The system for doing so was developed by Sir Edward Henry in 1896 and is still employed today. It divides fingerprint ridge patterns into four distinct groups:

Arches. In arches, the ridges span the finger from one side to another without interruption and without making a backward turn.

Loops. In loops, some ridges spanning the finger make a backward turn, but without a twist. Two out of every three ridge patterns will be a loop.

Whorls. Some of the ridges make a turn through at least one complete circuit. Whorls can be single or double cored.

Composites. Patterns in which combinations of the arch, loop, and whorl are found in the same print.

3. Compare the prints to those of your suspects. If a match is found, you can definitively connect that suspect to the scene or to a murder weapon. If not, you might stoop to collaborating with the local constabulary in order to compare your crime scene prints to those in a police database. Recidivism, after all, is common amongst the criminal element; if your suspect has been arrested before, his prints are likely to be in a police database.

Double Loop   Centered Loop   Arch Loop

Lateral Loop   Loop   Composite

Whorl   Arch

Scotland Yard

"We're not jealous of you at Scotland Yard. No, sir, we are very proud of you, and if you come down to-morrow there's not a man, from the oldest inspector to the youngest constable, who wouldn't be glad to shake you by the hand."

—Scotland Yard's Inspector Lestrade to Sherlock Holmes,

"The Six Napoleons"

 cotland Yard, as London's Metropolitan Police force is colloquially known, is neither in Scotland, nor is it a yard. The misnomer is thought to have been inspired by the location of its original London headquarters, which opened onto the courtyard of a medieval residence once owned by the Scottish royal family. As the force multiplied in size—from three thousand constables at its inception in 1829 to more than fourteen thousand by the turn of the next century—it outgrew the Yard and moved elsewhere, but retained the name.

The act of Parliament that created Scotland Yard was introduced by Home Secretary Sir Robert Peel, and it is after him that the "bobbies" who protect London are nicknamed. These "new police" gradually supplanted a number of smaller, independent policing organizations that had proved themselves insufficiently effective at keeping the peace in a rapidly changing city. (That didn't include the City of London police, which has existed in one form or another since Roman times and still operates within the one-square-mile city center.) Scotland Yard's bobbies were responsible for protecting important citizens, patrolling the streets, maintaining community relations, and managing their own personnel.

The highest-ranking officer was the commissioner and the lowest was the constable, the equivalent of a beat cop in the United States. Sergeants were in charge of a shift of constables and sometimes accompanied rookie constables (also known as "probationers") on patrol. The chief inspector managed all uniformed officers assigned to specific stations, which were spread throughout the boroughs of London.

The Criminal Investigation Department is a separate branch of Scotland Yard and was the one in which Holmes's sometime-allies, the inspectors Lestrade, Jones, and Gregson, would have worked. The department wasn't officially established until 1878; prior to that, only a few dozen plainclothes officers had been specifically assigned to the investigation of crimes. Although Londoners were at first suspicious—some regarded these under-cover officers as spies—the inspectors' value quickly became apparent once they had solved a number of high-profile crimes. As criminal activity in London dropped off noticeably through the end of the nineteenth century, Scotland Yard gradually gained the trust of a wary public.

Sherlock Holmes, on the other hand, was always skeptical of its inspectors' deductive powers: "Gregson is the smartest of the Scotland Yarders," Holmes observed in *A Study in Scarlet*. "He and Lestrade are the pick of a bad lot." Of his own unique position in the hierarchy of London law enforcement, Holmes said: "When Gregson or Lestrade or Athelney Jones are out of their depths—which, by the way, is their normal state—the matter is laid before me."

How to Analyze Typography

"It is a curious thing that a typewriter has really quite as much individuality as a man's handwriting."
—Sherlock Holmes, "A Case of Identity"

hen the Philo-Remington company began manufacturing typewriters for home and office use in 1873, handwriting analysts mourned the death of an era: Now criminals would use them to draft untraceable letters, they feared, hiding their identities behind the homogeneity of typewriter script. In "A Case of Identity," however, Sherlock Holmes proves that such fears were unfounded. The case concerns a young woman who hires Holmes to investigate the disappearance of her secretive fiancé, a man who jilted her at the altar after wooing her via typewritten letters. Holmes discovers at least fifteen subtle typographical characteristics of her lover's letters that match those of her stepfather's typewriter and concludes that the lover and stepfather are, in fact, the same person.

It seems the whole affair was a cruel scheme to prevent the young lady from marrying. Should you ever find yourself studying similar evidence, consider the following primer on typography analysis.

- **Examine characters for recurring abnormalities.** Unless a typewriter is absolutely new, Holmes says, "no two of them write exactly alike. Some letters get more worn than others, and some wear only on one side." Inexpensive machines may suffer alignment defects, regardless of their age. In the case of the cruel stepfather's typewriter—by no means a cheap model—Holmes detects "some little slurring over of the *e*, and a slight defect in the tail of the *r*," minor but observable hallmarks identical to abnormalities found in the fictional fiancé's letters.

My dear friend Sherlock Holmes

• **Check the depth of impression.** Until the electrical typewriter came into widespread use in the mid-twentieth century, some physical force was required for keystrokes to make an acceptably inky impression on paper. The depth of this impression depends entirely on the force applied, and thus a particularly aggressive typist's letters might be differentiated from those made with a lighter touch. In addition, depth of impression can vary perceptibly depending on the typewriter's model and manufacturer.

impression   impression

• **Measure the leading.** In the days when type was set by hand in printing presses, strips of lead were placed between the lines to separate them and could be varied in height to achieve different spacing. Thus, the measure of vertical space

between lines of type is known as *leading*. Not perfectly standardized in Holmes's day, leading differed slightly between
typewriters of different manufacturers and countries. You
probably won't convict anyone with leading evidence alone,
but it can prove invaluable when considered with other
typographical characteristics.

```
To deduce the          To deduce the
truth requires a       truth requires a
scrutinous obser-      scrutinous obser-
vation of the          vation of the
facts, and the         facts, and the
clarity to discern     clarity to discern
crucial details        crucial details
from a pack of         from a pack of
trivialities.          trivialities.
```

• **Inspect the typewriter ribbon.** Only the sloppiest of
criminals would neglect to burn a ribbon used to compose
an incriminating letter, but in those serendipitous cases in
which they do, any still-legible keystroke impressions that
can be gleaned from the used ribbon are invaluable. If a ribbon has been reused on multiple occasions, however—as
older cloth ribbons were meant to be—reading it may prove
impossible.

Be Aware

Few criminals possess an unerring command of the English language. Take heed of unique and recurring grammatical errors bound to appear in the prose of barely literate louts and Oxford-educated aristocrats alike.

221B Baker Street

So desirable in every way were the apartments, and so moderate did the terms seem when divided between us, that the bargain was concluded upon the spot, and we at once entered into possession.

—*A Study in Scarlet*

he modest rooms shared by Sherlock Holmes and Dr. Watson are surely one of literature's most famous fictional addresses. The circumstances of the pair's coming together as housemates could not have been more random: Having recently returned, wounded and exhausted, from military service in the British conflict in Afghanistan, Dr. Watson writes that he "naturally gravitated to London, that great cesspool into which all the loungers and idlers of the Empire are irresistibly drained." Living there in an overpriced hotel, friendless, and running out of money, the good doctor soon finds himself in dire financial straits. Quite by accident, he encounters an old

acquaintance from medical school with a friend who's looking
for someone to share rooms with—a queer fellow named
Sherlock Holmes—which seems a perfect solution to Watson's
troubles. Despite warnings about Holmes's bizarre personality, he
and Watson quickly agree to take up lodgings together at some
"nice rooms" that Holmes had found but were too dear for him
to rent alone. And so began their auspicious partnership and residence at 221B Baker Street.

Baker Street was a wide, busy thoroughfare in the
Marylebone district of London, rather a tony neighborhood for
two young men of limited means. The rooms are described in *A
Study in Scarlet*: "They consisted of a couple of comfortable bed-
rooms and a single large airy sitting room, cheerfully furnished,
and illuminated by two broad windows." It was a split-plan apartment, with Watson's bedroom above the sitting room and the
landlord Mrs. Hudson's below. There was a tree in a small yard
behind the house, and some trees lining Baker Street itself.

The somewhat claustrophobic sitting room was furnished
with a "humble lodging-house mahogany" breakfast table and
chairs, a plush armchair and wicker basket chair, sofa, sideboard, a
bearskin rug before a fireplace, and a little side table where
Holmes performed his noisome chemistry experiments. Watson
was the neater of the two men, a fact that occasionally becomes
a source of conflict; in "The Musgrave Ritual" the doctor com-

ments that Holmes is "one of the most untidy men that ever drove a fellow-lodger to distraction," noting his flatmate's habit of keeping "his tobacco in the toe end of a Persian slipper and his unanswered correspondence transfixed by a jack-knife into the very centre of his wooden mantelpiece." We also learn that Holmes is something of a pack rat whose "horror of destroying documents" and desperate lack of any coherent system of filing leads at one point to "every corner" of the Baker Street sitting room being "stacked with bundles of manuscript which were on no account to be burned, and which could not be put away save by their owner."

In reality, there never was a 221B Baker Street; when Doyle wrote the stories, Baker Street's numbers stopped at 100. German bombs destroyed much of the neighborhood during World War II, and though today the modern renumbered Baker Street goes well into the 200s, there is no 221B; a large art deco building was assigned the odd numbers from 219 to 229 in the 1930s. Still, that did not stop its tenants, the Abbey National Building Society, from receiving Holmes's mail—so much so that they were forced to appoint an employee to act as Holmes's personal secretary. Nikki Caparn, who served in this role in the late 1980s, told the *New York Times* that most of the detective's correspondents "just want to know what Mr. Holmes is doing now or where he is and they hope he is well," and she often responds in Holmes's own

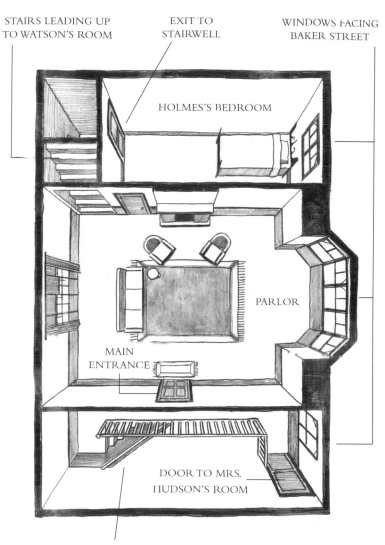

STAIRS LEADING UP
TO WATSON'S ROOM

EXIT TO
STAIRWELL

WINDOWS FACING
BAKER STREET

HOLMES'S BEDROOM

PARLOR

MAIN
ENTRANCE

DOOR TO MRS.
HUDSON'S ROOM

STAIRS TO BAKER STREET

FLOORPLAN OF 221B BAKER STREET

words, explaining that he has retired to the countryside and "given himself up entirely to that soothing life of nature for which I had so often yearned during the long years amid the gloom of London."

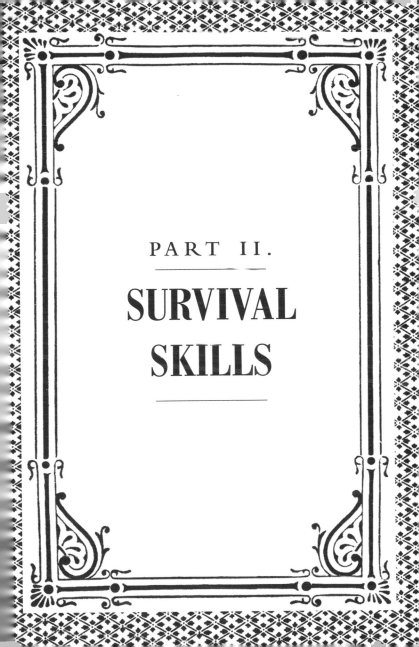

PART II.

SURVIVAL
SKILLS

How to Defend Yourself

"I don't think you can have forgotten me. Don't you remember the amateur who fought three rounds with you at Alison's rooms on the night of your benefit four years back?"

"Not Mr. Sherlock Holmes!" roared the prize-fighter . . . "If instead o' standin' there so quiet you had just stepped up and given me that crosshit of yours under the jaw, I'd ha' known you without a question. Ah, you're one that has wasted your gifts, you have!"

—*The Sign of the Four*

herlock Holmes might have been renowned for powers of mind, but he could hold his own in a fight just as handily as in a game of chess. He was an accomplished swordsman and singlestick fighter, a martial artist whose knowledge of Bartitsu saved his life at Reichenbach Falls in "The

Final Problem." And, according to Dr. Watson, he was "undoubtedly one of the finest boxers of his weight that I have ever seen."
This impressive breadth of knowledge preserved the great detective's life on many occasions, and if you would enjoy a long and
healthy career such as his, you must develop your powers of self-
defense as well as your powers of deduction.

1. Learn Bartitsu. Adapted from Jujitsu, the ancient
Japanese method of weaponless self-defense, Bartitsu—
named for its English progenitor, Mr. E. W. Barton-Wright—
is a martial art designed to turn the momentum of an opponent's attack against him. Holmes describes a classic move

from his infamous showdown with arch-nemesis Moriarty in "The Final Problem," in which Moriarty attempts to grab Holmes, but Holmes "slipped through his grip," knocking Moriarty off balance and sending him plunging over a waterfall to his death. Holmes's strategy is typical of most Bartitsu techniques: Use the momentum of your opponent's attack to disrupt his equilibrium, surprise him before he has time to regain his balance, and finally—unless you've already sent him plummeting over a waterfall—subject his joints to strain that they are anatomically unable to resist.

2. Use your fists. When Holmes's unwelcome inquiries provoke a bar fight in "The Solitary Cyclist," his boxing skills serve him well: "He ended a string of abuse by a vicious back-hander which I failed to entirely avoid," Holmes reports. "The next few minutes were delicious. It was a straight left against a slogging ruffian. I emerged as you see me; [my opponent] went home in a cart." In order to give a similar performance, be sure to keep your feet shoulder width apart, the dominant foot slightly behind the other. Hold your dominant fist close to your chin and your opposite a few inches from your face, elbow bent; this allows you to block incoming punches while waiting for the perfect opportunity to throw your own. Keep your body moving, shifting weight from foot to foot in a bouncing motion, which transforms you into a difficult-to-hit moving target. Combination punches are most effective, a common example being the jab-cross: a straight punch with your leading hand followed by a cross aimed at your opponent's face. Enhance the latter's power by shifting your weight forward while throwing the punch; with any luck, one successful combination is the only move you'll need.

3. Use a sword. Though Holmes never makes practical use of his sword-fighting skills in the canon, we do know he

studied fencing in college and was rated an expert swordsman by Dr. Watson. If he had faced off with a sword-wielding
opponent, therefore, we may assume Holmes would've used
some of the following expert techniques. Most important is
a strong defense: Hold your sword vertically, extended a
comfortable distance from your body while keeping your
elbows bent and close to your torso. This position allows you
to respond to attacks with maximum speed and minimum
unnecessary motion while providing many options for
launching strikes of your own. Maintain your balance at all
times, standing with feet at shoulder width and your chest

and torso slightly ahead of your waist. Stand no farther than one lunging step from your opponent, the length of which depends largely on the length of your sword. The head and upper body should be the primary focus of your attacks, but don't be afraid to strike at arms or legs; many a swordfight was won after an opponent fainted due to blood loss from superficial wounds.

4. Use a stick. In "The Illustrious Client," Holmes fends off a murderous attack by two men armed with sticks. When Watson demands to know how his friend escaped alive—if a bit worse for wear—Holmes reminds Watson that he is "a bit

of a singlestick expert" and explains that he fought back with his cane. Proper technique demands that the stick be held high in one hand, positioned horizontally so that it guards the head while maintaining a ready position. Stand in a wide stance three feet from your opponent, with your dominant foot forward and your opposite back. Direct strikes toward your opponent's head; body blows inflict comparatively little harm. Strikes aimed at the wrist may serve to disarm an opponent, putting him at your mercy.

The Sporting Life

"My ramifications stretch out into many sections of society, but never, I am happy to say, into amateur sport, which is the best and soundest thing in England. However . . . even in that world of fresh air and fair play there may be work for me to do."

—Sherlock Holmes, "The Missing Three-Quarter"

rthur Conan Doyle may have been a sporting man— he loved to play soccer and cricket, he shot billiards as well as rifles, and he piloted hot-air balloons, bicycles, and race cars—but his greatest creation, Sherlock Holmes, most emphatically is not. The detective's ego-driven temperament is such that rather than submit to the cooperative team play of a league, Holmes is drawn instead to activities that pit individual combatants against one another: boxing, sword fighting, and martial arts. But his author's love of sports pervades the stories nevertheless, and so Holmes's investigations frequently lead him onto the sports field despite his disdain for "fresh air and fair play."

Amongst the upper classes of Holmes's day, hunting was by far the most popular sport. Fox hunting, fishing and bird shooting all boasted enormous followings among the wealthy and privileged; as Samuel Johnson wrote, "Hunting was the labor of savages in America but the amusement of the gentlemen of England." We may assume that Holmes himself knows something of hunting: not only is he facile with guns, but he often carries a hunting crop with him. Used to control one's horse during a hunt, the crop in Holmes's hands was more often put to work controlling uncooperative suspects.

Second in popularity only to killing animals was racing them, and horseracing in particular was enjoyed by Victorians of every social strata. The difference was participatory: The wealthy owned, bred, and raced the horses while common folk served as enthusiastic spectators and bettors. Naturally, most of Holmes's clients were of the former persuasion, including Colonel Ross in the "Silver Blaze" case, in which Holmes is tasked to find the colonel's missing racehorse, Silver Blaze. He does, of course, and then deduces that the horse's late trainer was killed while trying to injure Silver Blaze in an effort to influence the outcome of a race for personal gain—and it was the horse's hoof blow to the head that did him in. Silver Blaze goes on to win a crucial race, on which Holmes slyly mentions that he "stands to win a little" money.

Team sports were loved by the Victorians, especially cricket, soccer, and rugby. Watson was a devoted rugby player—Holmes's client in "The Sussex Vampire" knew Watson from their youthful days as amateur players—and the sport figures prominently in "The Missing Three-Quarter" mystery. It hinges on a star rugby player, Godfrey Staunton (the titular "three-quarter"), who disappears just prior to an important match. The fact that Holmes has never heard of Staunton (nor, presumably, any other prominent rugby player) led one pair of astonished Sherlockian critics to propose that the great detective was actually a woman in disguise. Such ignorance on the part of any male who had attended public school in nineteenth-century England was unfathomable, they argue. Descended from soccer, rugby captured the popular imagination from the time players began to pick up the ball and run with it around 1830; and by 1872, when Cambridge officially institutionalized its rugby club as a sport distinct from soccer, it had become an inescapable part of the fabric of English society. Then again, perhaps Holmes, whose spirit rebelled against the gentlemanly values of selfless team play it was thought to instill in impressionable young men, simply blocked the whole business from his mind.

How to Outwit a Criminal Mastermind

"He is the Napoleon of crime, Watson. He is the organizer of half that is evil and of nearly all that is undetected in this great city. He is a genius, a philosopher, an abstract thinker. He has a brain of the first order."

—Sherlock Holmes describing Professor Moriarty in
"The Final Problem"

owerful minds are not always drawn to the pursuit of good; there are those whose genius is tainted with criminality and who, as Holmes believed of his arch-nemesis Professor Moriarty, possess "hereditary tendencies of the most diabolical kind." Like Holmes, you may discover that the crimes committed in your city are not the random work of unrelated thieves and killers but are connected—though subtly—in a giant web, at the center of which is a mastermind like Moriarty, controlling all from a seemingly untouchable remove. Until you can find proof admissible in a court of law that such is the case, however, your day-to-day casework will remain an unending, Sisyphean task; unless you can outwit the mastermind, your crime-solving efforts will address only the branches of evil, not the root. By undertaking the following methods, you may be able to take the fight to him.

1. Gather evidence of the mastermind's crimes. This first step is the most difficult, for as Holmes said of Moriarty, "so aloof is he from general suspicion . . . so admirable in his management and self-effacement" that finding proof of his criminal ties may seem impossible. Holmes's method was comprehensive: He surreptitiously searched Moriarty's house on three occasions (and found "absolutely nothing"), peeked into the mastermind's finances ("I made it my business to hunt down some of Moriarty's checks"), and tracked the doings of Moriarty's criminal associates. Most importantly, he took every precaution to conduct his investigations without the mastermind's knowledge; unfortunately, Holmes reports in "The Final Problem," Moriarty was "too wily for that." If you too are found out, proceed to the next step.

2. Thwart his attempts to assassinate you. "The only conceivable escape for him," said Holmes of his archenemy, "lay in silencing my tongue." Yet it's not from the mastermind himself that the blow likely will fall, but from one of his many agents, and it's in their interest to kill you quickly and quietly. That can only mean one thing: snipers. Holmes's prodigious paranoia of assassins wielding silent-but-deadly air guns in "The Final Problem" likely saves his life, as does his insistence on keeping clear of windows and closing all shutters. Do likewise, and in addition make yourself as difficult as possible to track, keeping to alleys and by-ways rather than main thoroughfares and using rear windows and garden walls to access buildings. Keep a revolver close at hand, but use it only if absolutely necessary, else you might end up in the dock for murder, rather than your enemy.

3. Make yourself scarce. Once your damning evidence has been assembled and the machinations of the mastermind's ruin are in motion, he will be at his most dangerous. Desperate, the mastermind will do anything to destroy you before the net of justice closes around him completely; it's prudent, therefore, to get as far away as possible until the game is won. Don a disguise, as Holmes did when Moriarty came after him in "The Final Problem," and hop the next train out of town. Tell no one save your most trusted confidant of your plans, for your enemy has spies everywhere. Travel light but leave nothing behind that you cannot live without—a lesson that Holmes and Watson learned the hard way when Moriarty's henchmen set fire to their famed Baker Street rooms as they fled.

4. Resist the temptation to have the mastermind arrested prematurely. Certainly the mastermind's desperate, last-minute attempts to assault you will involve a few arrestable offenses, but these are petty crimes compared to the vast network of felonies in which he has had a hand. Bide your time or risk watching him tried for an offense against which his powerful lawyers can easily defend while his henchmen go free, swearing vengeance against you. Or, as Holmes explained the dilemma to Watson, "We should get the big fish, but the smaller would dart right and left out of the net."

5. Don't let down your guard. He will eventually find you, of that you can be certain; all you can do is delay the inevitable showdown. Lest he should take you by surprise, adopt an attitude of hyper-vigilance, as Watson describes Holmes doing: "I could tell by his quick glancing eyes and his sharp scrutiny of every face that passed us, he was well convinced that, walk where we would, we could not walk ourselves clear of the danger that was dogging our footsteps."

6. Prepare for the final assault. The mastermind will attack when he thinks you're most vulnerable. You must let him do it, but be ready. In "The Final Problem," Holmes and Watson flee London for the tiny Swiss hamlet of Meiringen and are trekking to see the fearful Reichenbach Falls when a messenger boy arrives with an urgent plea for Dr. Watson: A woman is dying at the hotel and needs Watson's attention. Though it's clear to Holmes that the boy is in Moriarty's employ and his plea is nothing but a thinly veiled scheme to get Holmes alone in a dangerous locale, Holmes goes along with it; the showdown must happen, and he is ready.

7. Fake your own death. This step assumes that you have succeeded in besting the mastermind in the previous step, as Holmes did Moriarty at Reichenbach Falls. After using martial artistry to send Moriarty plunging to his death, Holmes finds himself confronted by a unique problem: He has succeeded in ridding the world of a criminal mastermind, yet his own life is in more danger than ever. Moriarty's henchmen remain free, and they will surely seek revenge. To return to

London would mean facing assassination at their hands, and traveling under his own name would mean pursuit by those same would-be assassins. He's forced to choose between facing death or feigning death and so opts for the latter, traveling far and wide for three years under an invented identity.

Will the Real Moriarty Please Stand Up?

ust as Sir Arthur based certain aspects of Sherlock Holmes on the author's own medical school mentor, Dr. Joseph Bell, there has been much speculation that Holmes's nemesis, arch-criminal professor Moriarty, was also based on an actual personage. Just who that criminal mastermind was, however, has long been a matter of debate. These are some of the most likely suspects.

• **Jonathan Wild, 1683–1725.** In *The Valley of Fear*, Holmes himself compares Moriarty to Jonathan Wild: "He was a master criminal . . . the hidden force of the London criminals, to whom he sold his brains and his organization on a fifteen per cent commission." Wild was born to "poor and respectable"

parents in the English countryside, but by his early twenties was consorting with prostitutes and thieves as part of London's thriving criminal underworld. He was responsible for one of the most notorious and successful criminal schemes in British history: An assistant to one of the city's most powerful (and corrupt) policemen, Wild controlled a gang of thieves who surreptitiously turned all their booty over to him. When the victims approached the police for help, Wild would announce that he had recovered their stolen goods and return them to their rightful owners for a reward (presumably to cover the expense of their retrieval). If any of his thieves ran afoul of him, he could simply have them arrested—and collect another reward for their capture. Thus, he ingeniously controlled and profited from much of London's crime while simultaneously taking credit for fighting it.

Much the same, Holmes characterizes Moriarty's gang as "a deep organizing power which forever stands in the way of the law, and throws its shield over the wrong-doer." What Holmes says of Moriarty himself could easily be said of Wild: "He does little himself. He only plans. But his agents are numerous and splendidly organized." Yet while Moriarty met his end at the bottom of Reichenbach Falls, Wild's death was more ignominious: So certain was he of his invulnerability to detection or prosecution that he began to carry a scepter with him and referred to himself as "The Thief-Taker General." His pretentious behavior and increasingly public persona only hastened his undoing, and Wild was found out and finally hanged before a capacity crowd in 1725. He inspired generations of writers even before Arthur Conan Doyle may or may not have used him as a template for Moriarty: Daniel Defoe witnessed his hanging and wrote newspaper articles about him, and in 1743 Henry Fielding wrote a satiric novel about him entitled *The Life and Death of Jonathan Wild, the Great.*

• **Adam Worth.** "He is the Napoleon of crime," Holmes says of Moriarty in "The Final Problem," a moniker that a real detective, Scotland Yard's Robert Anderson, had famously given to a real criminal, Adam Worth, some years earlier. German by birth, Worth's parents moved the family to Massachusetts when he was five years old. Just seventeen when the Civil War broke out in 1860, Worth lied about his age and joined the Union Army. He was wounded in the Second Battle of Bull Run two years later but was listed as killed in action, a mistake that worked to his advantage as he used his sudden anonymity to embark upon a life of crimes committed under assumed names.

Soon thereafter he founded a gang of pickpockets and thieves in New York City. He was caught, but escaped from Sing Sing prison after serving just a few weeks of a three-year sentence, and began organizing bank robberies. In 1869 he broke *into* a prison in order to free the notorious safecracker Charley Bullard, who then teamed with Worth to stage a stunning bank robbery via underground tunnel (which may have inspired the attempted bank robbery via tunnel in Conan Doyle's "The Red-Headed League"). With the police in hot pursuit, the pair decided to move their criminal endeavors to Europe.

They robbed pawnshops in Liverpool, ran a bar that was a front for a gambling den in Paris (the gaming tables could be folded into the floor during police raids), fenced stolen diamonds from South Africa, and organized a major criminal network in London. Like Moriarty, Worth rarely committed any of the robberies himself, and most of the people working for him didn't even know his name. Worth eventually slipped up and was captured in 1892, but police could only prove his involvement in a single robbery, for which he was sentenced to seven years and released early for good behavior in 1897. He recounted his life story to an agent of Pinkerton Detective Agency—his old nemesis—and retired to London to spend the remainder of his days in comfort with his children.

Besides Holmes's "Napoleon of crime" reference, Conan Doyle gives us one additional clue that Moriarty may have been based on Adam Worth. Worth admitted to having personally stolen an extremely valuable Thomas Gainsborough painting from London's Agnew & Sons gallery—not to fence it, but simply because he admired it. Gainsborough's portrait of Georgiana Cavendish, Duchess of Devonshire, hung in Worth's home for a number of years. In *The Valley of Fear*, Holmes notes that Moriarty owned a painting called *La Jeune Fille à l'Agneau*, a clever play on the name of the gallery from which Worth's Gainsborough was purloined.

• **Astronomers and mathematicians.** In addition to being a criminal genius, Moriarty was a luminary of the mathematics world. "His career has been an extraordinary one," Holmes says. "At the age of twenty-one he wrote a treatise upon the Binomial Theorem, which has had a European vogue. On the strength of it he won the Mathematical Chair at one of our smaller universities, and had, to all appearance, a most brilliant career before him." Of course, the professor's diabolical tendencies prevented him from being a wholly productive member of society, and his brilliant career quickly became a sideline to dark dealings in London's criminal underworld.

Though Adam Worth and Jonathan Wild fit the Moriarty mold in many ways, neither were mathematicians, a fact that has led some Holmes scholars still further afield in search of Moriarty's true model. Some have speculated that Moriarty resembles the American astronomer Simon Newcomb, one of America's foremost scientists in the decades following the Civil War. A brilliant polymath who authored groundbreaking studies of the heavenly bodies as well as books on economics, statistics, and even a science-fiction novel, Newcomb was also a notoriously outspoken partisan with a nasty personal reputation. A contemporary described him as a "dynamic and intimidating individual . . . more feared than liked."

Holmes also credits Moriarty with being "the celebrated author of *The Dynamics of an Asteroid*, a book that ascends to such rarefied heights of pure mathematics that it is said there was no man in the scientific press capable of criticizing it." The German mathematician Carl Freidrich Gauss authored a much-lauded paper on the dynamics of an asteroid that, like Moriarty, helped him earn a professorship. Other candidates mentioned have been George Boole (1815–1864), inventor of an algebra that serves as the basis of modern computer algorithms, and Indian mathematician Srinivasa Ramanujan (1887–1920), an untrained genius whose work on the binomial theorem found, as Holmes said of Moriarty, "no man in the scientific press capable of criticizing."

Like Sherlock Holmes, Professor Moriarty's powers are just superhuman enough that perhaps no man could serve as a true model. He is, therefore, a composite: He has the criminal cunning of Jonathan Wild, the untouchable suaveness of mastermind Adam Worth, and the irascible genius of Newcomb, Gauss, and Ramanujan. Consider the world fortunate that no such man could ever truly exist.

How to Fake Your Own Death

"I owe you many apologies, dear Watson, but it was all-important that it should be thought I was dead, and it is quite certain that you would not have written so convincing an account of my unhappy end had you not yourself thought that it was true."

—Sherlock Holmes, "The Empty House"

ny consulting detective as successful as Sherlock Holmes is sure to rack up an impressive list of powerful enemies, and sometimes—as Holmes decided was the case in "The Final Problem"—the best way to escape their vengeance is to fake one's own death. This is by no means an option for the faint of heart. Not only is it a cruel thing to inflict upon those who care for you, but it requires an exceeding amount of bother to execute the deed properly. Pray that you never have to embark upon the steps outlined here!

1. Design a persuasive death scene. The best kind—and your only option, really—is a death that leaves no recognizable body behind. Explosions or fires are good choices, provided you plant a skeleton in the wreckage that may plausibly be identified as your own. Water-related tragedies in which the corpse is unrecoverable are also ideal, as was Holmes's choice in "The Final Problem"—he made it appear as though he'd tumbled over the lofty Reichenbach Falls, the treacherous bottom of which authorities didn't even bother to search for his remains. Holmes's footprints led up to the precipice and disappeared, leading all concerned to conclude he had fallen to his death—when in fact he had merely climbed over a nearby ledge, where he hid until the scene was deserted and he could make a stealthy escape.

2. Skip town. As long as you remain near your old familiar haunts or anyone who might recognize you, you're in danger. Get as far as possible from your home and the scene of your "death," as quickly as you can. When Holmes miraculously returns to London in "The Empty House," he tells Watson about the exotic places he'd lived in the intervening three years: Tibet, Persia, Mecca, and Egypt, among other distant locales. Those were extreme choices, to be sure, but extraordinarily safe ones—the chances of his meeting someone there whom he had known prior to his "death" were low indeed.

3. Assume a new identity. Though your body lives on, your former identity must die. Grow facial hair, change your walk, and develop a new accent to help bury obvious traces of your former self. While traveling far and wide, Holmes went undercover as a Norwegian explorer named Sigerson, whose exploits and discoveries were fantastic enough to make international headlines. Yet he was never recognized as Holmes himself, so convincing was this disguise.

4. Arrange access to a supply of money. Travel is expensive, and you'll no longer have access to bank accounts or lines of credit established under your real name. You can

always bring cash with you or deposit money into an anony-
mous offshore account, but keep in mind that making any
sudden, last-minute transfers or withdrawals into that
account before your death is extremely suspect behavior. If
you're able to plan your death significantly in advance, make
gradual, monthly transfers over a period of several years to
avoid suspicion. Less advisable was Holmes's technique: He
revealed himself to his brother Mycroft, who became
Holmes's sole confidant and source of funds. Had Mycroft
been compromised in some way, Holmes's secret would've
been revealed, and his life put into considerable danger.
Which brings us to the next point:

5. Reveal yourself to no one. The wrenching heartache
endured by your loved ones is your enemies' most convincing proof you're really dead. Should their grief-stricken ulu-
lations seem forced or overly theatrical, someone is sure to
smell a rat. This profound separation from friends and relations will undoubtedly be the most trying aspect of your
ordeal, as even cold and logical Holmes admits—"Several
times during the past three years I have taken up my pen to
write to you," he apologizes to Watson—but such cruel
alienation is necessary. Holmes explains why: "I feared your
affectionate regard for me should tempt you to some indis-

cretion which would betray my secret."

6. Wait until your enemies are at their weakest to return. With time, the fires of your enemies' vengeance will cool, and their guard will fall. They may themselves die or be jailed (for such are dangers of the criminal life) and when they are at their most defenseless, as Holmes judged his to be shortly before his dramatic resurrection, it's time to return home.

7. Minimize the shock to your friends and family. When Holmes finally reveals himself to Watson, he does it in such a shocking way—which Holmes himself later confesses was "unnecessarily dramatic"—that poor Watson, a veteran of war and a man of sound constitution, faints on the spot. Imagine the effect such an appearance would have on the elderly or the anxious, and do your all to introduce yourself to them gradually. Save surprising flourishes for your enemies!

The Great Hiatus

"Poor Holmes is dead and damned."

—Arthur Conan Doyle, 1896

rthur Conan Doyle owed much of his career and literary reputation to Sherlock Holmes, but just a few years after introducing the great detective to the world in 1887's A Study in Scarlet, Doyle was already sick of his greatest creation. In an 1891 letter to his mother, Doyle admits to entertaining thoughts of "slaying Holmes . . . and winding him up for good," though it would be another two years—and two collections of iconic Holmes stories—before Doyle made good on his threat.

"The Final Problem," of 1893, was a shock to Holmes fans the world over. In it, the great detective apparently meets his end at the hands of his arch-nemesis Professor Moriarty, both of whom Watson believes have tumbled to their deaths over Switzerland's notorious Reichenbach Falls, where "will lie for all time the most dangerous criminal and the foremost champion of the law of their generation." Men wore black armbands in the streets of London and subscriptions plummeted to the magazine in which Doyle's Holmes stories appeared, but Doyle himself seemed to breathe a sigh of relief. Explaining his decision to a heartbroken public a few years later, he wrote:

> *I have had such an overdose of [Holmes] that I feel*
> *towards him as I do towards pâté de foie gras, of which I*
> *once ate too much, so that the name of it gives me a sickly*
> *feeling to this day. . . . I have been much blamed for doing*
> *that gentleman to death, but I hold that it was not mur-*
> *der, but justifiable self-defence, since, if I had not killed*
> *him, he would certainly have killed me.*

Try as he might to keep the detective locked in his watery grave, however, Holmes refused to stay there forever. Perhaps Doyle's repulsion toward him had waned over time, or the financial promise of pulling the dust-covers from 221B Baker Street had proved irresistible; whatever Doyle's reasoning, Holmes finally reappeared in 1901, eight years after "The Final Problem" had seemingly killed him, in *The Hound of the Baskervilles*. Doyle was showered with adulation for the now-classic tale, but the public still wasn't satisfied; he had set Baskervilles before the events of "The Final Problem," leaving the world's favorite detective still theoretically posthumous.

Responding to pressure from friends and fans, Doyle finally brought Holmes back from the dead in 1903 with "The Adventure of the Empty House," which finds Holmes back in London after three years of exile, explaining to an astonished Watson that he'd been forced to fake his death in order to elude

Moriarty's vengeful henchmen. Doyle would write three more collections of Holmes mysteries over the next twenty-four years, but fans and scholars continue to puzzle over the detective's period of mysterious exile, known as "The Great Hiatus," and what might've taken place during it. Of course, Holmes himself tells Watson where he's been in "The Empty House"—for two years he explored such far-flung lands as Tibet and Persia under the guise of a "Norwegian named Sigerson" before moving to France, Holmes says, where he conducted laboratory research on "coal-tar derivatives." Hearing that his enemies in London were in a weakened state (and intrigued by news of a new mystery he might help solve), Holmes finally returned to Baker Street.

But this wasn't enough for many Holmes fans, who had their own ideas about the Great Hiatus. Nicholas Meyer's novel *The Seven-Per-Cent Solution* supposes that Holmes spent his hiatus years recovering from cocaine addiction under the care of Sigmund Freud. Other drug-related hiatus theories range from Holmes traveling to Tibet to grow opium to spending his time there studying Buddhism in an effort to kick his habit. More skeptical readers wondered if Holmes had ever left London at all and whether the entire "hiatus" was a scheme cooked up by Watson to deceive Moriarty's henchmen; others suggested that Holmes may actually have died at Reichenbach Falls and been replaced by a convincing imposter. A less outlandish school of thought holds that Holmes had married Irene Adler—the beautiful opera singer from "A Scandal in Bohemia" who was, famously, one of the few persons ever to outwit the detective—and that the "hiatus" was really their extended honeymoon.

The world may never know.

How to Survive a Plunge over a Waterfall

"It was not a pleasant business, Watson. The fall roared
beneath me . . . a mistake would have been fatal."
—Sherlock Holmes, "The Empty House"

or three long years, poor Dr. Watson believed that his great friend and partner, Sherlock Holmes, had perished with his arch-enemy Moriarty in Switzerland's vertiginous Reichenbach Falls. But the tragic events of "The Final Problem" proved to be somewhat less than final in the subsequent "Adventure of the Empty House," in which Holmes reappears, much to Watson's delight and surprise, disguised as a wizened old book collector. Recovering from the shock, Watson's curiosity soon gets the best of him: "Sit down and tell me how you came alive out of that dreadful chasm!" he demands. Holmes's slightly flip answer reveals the simplest way to survive such a fall: not to fall at all. "I had no serious difficulty in getting out of it," he says, "for the very simple reason that I never was in it." But if your luck vis-à-vis waterfalls and the laws of gravity aren't as robust as the great detective's, do not despair. Here are a few techniques that may yet save your life.

- **Take a deep breath before you fall.** The trip down will be quick, unpleasant, and very wet; any breaths you draw after having left the precipice will likely fill your lungs with water. Remember, it may be some time before you're able to breathe again, and when you enter the river below, air-filled lungs will make you more buoyant.

- **Jump out, away from the edge.** If possible, leap as far from the ledge as you can. There may be a rocky outcropping you very much want to avoid on the way down, as well as boulders, which tend to accumulate in the water directly below waterfalls. As a general rule, the farther from the ledge you jump, the deeper the water will be in which you'll land.

• **Keep your body vertical, feet pointing down.** It's impossible to know how deep the water is, so it's safest to jump feet-first. Should you break your feet and legs, you may still be able to reach the shore; breaking your skull is another matter. Neither is it advisable to land on your back, which will shatter like a cheap wine decanter.

• **Use your arms to protect your head.** As Holmes said in "The Mazarin Stone," "I am a brain, Watson. The rest of me is mere appendix." Therefore, of your anatomical parts that may sustain damage in the fall—your limbs, rump, genitalia, or cranium—it's this last that is of paramount importance to protect. Wrap your arms around your head to shield it from unyielding objects encountered during your fall.

• **Spread your arms and legs when you enter the water.** This will create drag and retard your descent.

• **Begin swimming immediately.** Time is not on your side. If the water is frigid, you may have less than thirty seconds to make it to shore before your muscles cramp and you enter a state of hypothermic shock. Paddle away from the falling water to avoid becoming trapped behind the waterfall, and head for the nearest strand of visible shoreline.

"IT IS [NOT] ADVISABLE TO LAND ON YOUR BACK, WHICH
WILL SHATTER LIKE A CHEAP WINE DECANTER."

Be Aware

Just because you've made it to shore doesn't mean the danger is at an end. Depending on wounds you may have sustained or the temperature of the water in which you were just immersed, you may be in need of rescue. While waiting for help to arrive, be sure to keep your shirt and trousers on. Though it may seem odd, many disoriented hypothermia victims will disrobe—a phenomenon known as paradoxical undressing—which only hastens potentially fatal temperature loss.

Curious Maladies and Quack Medicines of the Victorian Era

Even the knowledge that he had succeeded where the police of three countries had failed, and that he had outmaneuvered at every point the most accomplished swindler in Europe, was insufficient to rouse him from his nervous prostration.

—Watson writing of Holmes, "The Reigate Squires"

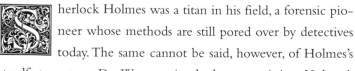 herlock Holmes was a titan in his field, a forensic pioneer whose methods are still pored over by detectives today. The same cannot be said, however, of Holmes's steadfast partner Dr. Watson; simply by committing Holmes's

many exploits to paper, Watson's contributions to literature far outstripped those of his undistinguished medical career. In the good doctor's defense, however, he can hardly be blamed for the strange diagnoses he sometimes reached or the cures he prescribed— *copious amounts of brandy!*—which were all common to the medical science of his age. They do, however, deserve some brief examination.

- **Nervous prostration** was a debilitating type of depressive exhaustion thought to be caused by the "intemperate exercise of the intellectual faculties." If Holmes sounds like a prime candidate for such a malady, indeed he was—as were such delicate thinkers as poetess Emily Dickinson, diagnosed with it a few years prior to her death in 1886. In "The Reigate Squires," Watson reports that Holmes's case of nervous prostration is a nasty one, characterized by "the blackest depression" from "the strain caused by his immense exertions in the spring of '87" (a case about which we know virtually nothing). Popular cures included beef tea, profound quiet, and extended vacations to the country, the latter two of which Watson prescribes to his old friend. After a mere week away from the harassing struggle of life in London, Holmes is feeling himself again and ready to tackle the "Reigate Squires" case.

• **Brain fever** was attributed to the "overindulgence of the passions" or a sudden emotional shock and is characterized by high fever and delirium. In "The Cardboard Box," the arrival by post of a pair of severed ears triggers a spinster's attack of brain fever. Holmes's client in "The Naval Treaty" has suffered "nine weeks of brain-fever" due to the theft of an important document. The condition, referred to nowadays as either encephalitis or meningitis, is known to be a swelling of the brain caused by bacterial infection, not heartbreak.

• **Leprosy** is no longer the hyper-contagious death sentence it was thought to be in Holmes's day. In "The Blanched Soldier," a young veteran is thought to have contracted the dread disease simply by sleeping in a leper's bed. He tells the tale with all requisite horror: "A chill came over me as I looked at them. Not one of them was a normal human being. Every one was twisted or swollen or disfigured in some strange way. The laughter of these strange monstrosities was a dreadful thing to hear." In fact, leprosy is *not* highly contagious; the *Mycobacterium leprae* that causes it is an organism particularly difficult to transmit. Effective drug treatments were developed in the 1930s and continue to improve. The forced quarantine of lepers since biblical times has been an unnecessary and regrettable cruelty.

• **Brandy** was regarded as something of an all-purpose restorative in Holmes's day, evidenced by episodes such as the one from "The Lion's Mane" in which an ill man stumbles into Holmes's room, "pallid, dishevelled, his clothes in wild disorder, clawing with his bony hands at the furniture to hold himself erect. 'Brandy! Brandy!' he gasped, and fell groaning upon the sofa." The afflicted man is quickly fed "a whole bottleful" of the spirit, whereupon Holmes reports that "it seems to have saved his life." Although modern medicine holds that brandy may benefit drinkers as a minor source of antioxidants, there is scant proof of its life-saving capabilities.

• **Patent medicines**, which numbered more than a thousand in Holmes's day, claimed they could do everything from prolong life to purify the blood and cure depression. The derogatory term "snake oil salesman" refers to the hucksters who peddled these cures, many of which contained alcohol and opiates as their active ingredients—and a few of which proved fatal. Watson himself never prescribed any, however, and Holmes's attitude toward such quackery is relayed in *The Sign of the Four* by his landlady, Mrs. Hudson: "I hope he's not going to be ill, sir. I ventured to say something to [Mr. Holmes] about cooling medicine, but he turned on me, sir, with such a look that I don't know how ever I got out of the room."

How to Disguise Yourself

It was not merely that Holmes changed his costume. His expression, his manner, his very soul seemed to vary with every fresh part that he assumed. The stage lost a fine actor, even as science lost an acute reasoner, when he became a specialist in crime.

— A Scandal in Bohemia

herlock Holmes was more than just a shrewd detective—among other distinctions, he remains one of history's foremost masters of disguise. His profession demanded it: Concealing his identity allowed Holmes to trail suspects without their knowledge, slip his enemies' traps time after time, and in "His Last Bow" to break a German spy ring that might have cost England dearly if not for Holmes's undercover intervention. That Dr. Watson himself failed to recognize his old friend in disguise on at least five occasions is further proof of Holmes's genius; and considering that Watson was a sharp if underrated mind in his own right, it goes without saying that Holmes's efforts went much further than simply donning a costume. To master the art of personal camouflage, every aspect of your person, from your clothes and hair to the manner in which you speak and carry yourself, must be altered beyond recognition.

• **Select a new identity.** You will fool no one by simply donning exotic clothes willy-nilly; a disguise lacking in coherence appears to be just what it is—a disguise. Instead, think like an actor: Imagine a character most unlike yourself and let that guide your selection of clothing, the manner in which you speak, the cover story you concoct, and so on. Consider the sex, age, profession, economic status, and personality of this character, as Holmes did when he disguised himself as an aged seaman in *The Sign of the Four* : "Altogether he gave me the impression of a respectable master mariner who had fallen into years and poverty," reports a briefly duped Watson.

• **Change your clothes.** In his career, Holmes wore a black robe and hat to become an Italian priest in "The Final Problem," a "blue blouse" to portray a rough-edged French plumber in "The Disappearance of Lady Frances Carfax," and a tweed suit and cloth hat to appear like "any other tourist" in *The Hound of the Baskervilles*, among many other costumes. But

Holmes does more than simply take these clothes from the rack and drape them on his person; he adapts them to the subtleties of his roles. For instance, his aged sailor costume in *The Sign of the Four* consisted mainly of a pea-coat, but it wasn't just any pea-coat: Watson describes it as "old" and "buttoned up to his throat," touches that reinforce both the poverty and infirmity of the character Holmes is playing.

• **Change your hair**. Holmes's sailor disguise employed not only a wig but fake whiskers and eyebrows as well, creating the impression of an unkempt man rarely acquainted with scissors or a razor. But false hair can be dangerous; nothing will ruin your cover more quickly than an ill-fitting wig.

• **Change your face.** This can be achieved by artificial means—with makeup to create wrinkles or flesh-colored putty to reshape the nose—as well as naturally, through facial expressions. For maximum effect, employ both techniques simultaneously, as Holmes does in "The Final Problem": "The aged ecclesiastic had turned his face towards me," Watson writes. "For an instant the wrinkles were smoothed away, the nose drew away from the chin, the lower lip ceased to protrude and the mouth to mumble . . . and the next the whole frame collapsed again, and Holmes had gone as quickly as he had come." He takes a different approach in "The Dying Detective," affecting the look of a man on his deathbed by applying petroleum jelly to his forehead, daubing his eyes with irritating nightshade to turn them angry red, and encrusting beeswax around his lips.

• **Change your body.** Desperate fools might submit to a surgeon's knife in order to change their bodies, but for a master of disguise, such measures are superfluous. Your natural stride should be lengthened or shortened, or a limp adopted. Holmes often altered his height by stooping while in disguise, a wonderful trick but no easy thing to maintain over a long period, as he pointed out after portraying a hunched bookseller in "The Empty House"—"I am glad to stretch myself, Watson," said Holmes. "It is no joke when a tall man has to take a foot off his stature for several hours on end."

• **Alter your speech.** An accent is easy enough to fake, but a new *manner* of speech is considerably more difficult. The most elaborate role of Holmes's career was that of an Irish American traitor named Altamont in "His Last Bow," whose voice alone was enough to convince the Germans on whom he was spying of his authenticity. "If you heard him talk you would not doubt [that he is Irish American]," Von Bork

"SHERLOCK HOLMES REMAINS ONE OF HISTORY'S
FOREMOST MASTERS OF DISGUISE."

assures a German comrade. "Sometimes I assure you I can hardly understand him. He seems to have declared war on the King's English as well as on the English king."

• **Make liberal use of props.** Props are an actor's best friend, and Holmes—who might have ruled the stage had he not become a detective—employs them at every opportunity. As a bookseller in "The Empty House," he carries an armful of heavy books. The Irish traitor Altamont holds a "half-smoked, sodden cigar" dangling from his lips at all times. Posing as fishermen, Holmes and Watson carry "a formidable litter of rods, reels, and baskets." So long as your props are consistent with the nature of the character you are portraying, they are a boon to any disguise.

BE AWARE

Depending on how long you're required to remain undercover, it may become challenging to stay constantly in character. But because you never know who might be watching, the most insignificant slip could prove fatal. Holmes, who immersed himself in the world of spies and assumed identities during the years prior to the events of "His Last Bow," makes reference to an undercover agent who hadn't the psychological timber for the job and "went bughouse when he had to play a part from morning to night." Only assume an identity, therefore, if you're certain you can commit to it.

Victorian Fashion

lthough the extreme formality of the early Victorian period had begun to slacken somewhat in Holmes's day, making way for slightly more comfortable styles of dress, the streets of London remained a sea bobbing with tall hats balanced atop sober dark-coated gentlemen and ladies whose breathing was so restricted by strangulating corsets that they dared not exert themselves for fear of fainting. Although Sir Arthur doesn't exert much authorial energy describing fashion—his and Holmes's preoccupations lie elsewhere—we know that the detective dressed as an urbane gentleman of London would have been expected to: He often wore a tall felt hat, though sometimes it was traded for a cloth traveling cap or a bowler, which had become an acceptable alternative to the otherwise ubiquitous top hat by the turn of the century. He was rarely without a tie, a waistcoat, and a knee-length frock coat and frequently carried an umbrella, which doubled as a weapon on at least one occasion.

So style conscious were the Victorians that even the poorest Londoners wore bonnets or hats, often salvaged used from middle-class owners and worn until they fell to pieces. Carpenters wore tailcoats, and omnibus conductors, policemen, postmen, and other working people wore tall black hats. Only the lowliest of laborers went about bare headed. As a result, there was a thriving market for second-hand clothes, many of which had been worn for years and rarely washed. (Bathing, tooth-brushing, and clothes-washing were rare luxuries for the Victorians, who instead took a mighty interest in colognes and perfumes.) The miasmatic stench of second-hand clothes markets was said to be overpowering.

In addition to a tall hat, the middle-class Victorian male habitually wore dark trousers, a coat, a waistcoat, and, in especially cold weather, an overcoat. Shirts were made either at home or by one's tailor and featured removable cuffs and collars that could easily be replaced if they became soiled or sweat stained. (The shirt itself, however—invisible beneath one's frock coat—could be worn for days or weeks on end.)

Women's fashion, then as ever, was considerably more elaborate and uncomfortable. In striving to achieve a perfect "hourglass" figure, Victorian women endured long, tightly laced corsets, cage-shaped crinolines that could support dresses up to six feet in diameter but made everyday activities like sitting or maneuvering through doorways humorously difficult (and that even Queen Victoria decried as "indelicate, expensive, dangerous and hideous"), heavy bustles that effectively created a two-foot shelf extending out from a lady's hindquarters, high heels, and vertigo-inducting hairstyles. For much of the Victorian era, a dress that dared to reveal the ankles of its wearer was considered the garb of prostitutes, and trousers for women were downright unthinkable.

Despite protests from clothing-reform advocates such as the Rational Dress Society (which in 1888 made the outrageous demand that the maximum weight of a woman's undergarments should "not exceed seven pounds"), it was the bicycle craze of the 1890s that did the most to liberalize women's fashion.

Because riding a bicycle was impossible (not to say dangerous) in a full-length skirt, the scandalous advent of cycling amongst strong-willed women eventually led to shorter skirts and even bifurcated garments called bloomers. Suddenly, women were able to pedal significant distances on their own, all while wearing less than seven pounds of underwear. Little wonder that Susan B. Anthony remarked that bicycling "had done more to emancipate women than anything else in the world."

Though they may not have washed their clothes very often, the Victorians did change them frequently—often several times per day. Women wore a morning dress in the daytime and for dinner donned lavish evening dresses that revealed their shoulders. A man might have worn one coat to breakfast and another to work, and yet another when smoking or walking in the park, and both men and women owned separate outfits for activities like riding, playing tennis, or going to the country. The class system was a strictly adhered-to facet of Victorian society, and the manner in which one dressed was an instant identifier of social position.

How to Cover Your Tracks

Holmes: "I followed you."
Suspect: "I saw no one."
Holmes: "That is what you may expect to see when
I follow you."

—"The Adventure of the Devil's Foot"

 n the science of physics, it's a well-known phenomenon that the act of observing may itself change that which is being observed. The same phenomenon is demonstrable in detective work: It is always preferable that the detective observe unobserved, lest a suspect redouble his efforts to remain hidden and the task at hand be compromised. When appropriate, therefore, consider applying the following obfuscational techniques.

- **Disguise your identity.** With luck, a convincing and frequently changing disguise will prevent suspects from realizing they are being shadowed. Disguises are especially vital for celebrated detectives whose features may be well known to the public; ever since Watson began writing about Holmes's cases, Holmes complains in *The Sign of the Four,* he "can only go on the war-path under some simple disguise" for fear of being recognized.

• **Disguise your footprints.** It's more than just detectives who excel at reading tracks and boot prints. To thwart those who may be following you, avoid walking in mud, soft grass, or other easy-to-track media. Carry a spare set of shoes of a size too small or large for your foot. By changing into them mid-journey, it will appear that you have left the path and a stranger has taken your place. Also consider reversing your shoes and wearing them rearward, as Holmes describes in "The Empty House," so those tracking you won't know if you are coming or going. (Though effective, keep in mind that this technique will slow your progress markedly.)

• **Disguise your intellect.** A suspect who believes he is in little danger of being found out is considerably less likely to flee. Because criminals tend to return to the scene of their crimes, while you are examining the location it is safest to operate under the assumption that you are also being watched by the criminal. Refrain from boastful declarations regarding your deductive prowess or the elementary nature of the case at hand, maintaining instead an appearance of frustration and befuddlement.

• **Sneak, skulk, and steal.** Make liberal use of rear entrances and garden walls, over which a fit detective should be able to scramble. Develop your knowledge of metropolitan alleyways, side streets, and tunnel systems—"It is a hobby of mine to have an exact knowledge of London," Holmes boasts in "The Red-Headed League"—and travel by them in favor of major thoroughfares, whenever possible.

• **Silence your shoes.** The acoustic propagation of your footfalls may be dampened by gluing felt or soft rubber to the soles of your shoes. Or simply wear shoes that are naturally dampened, as Holmes advises Watson to do when sneaking into the home of a notorious blackmailer in "Charles Augustus Milverton." "I have a pair of rubber-soled tennis shoes," Watson says. "Excellent," replies Holmes.

PART III.

LIFE SKILLS

How to Stage a Dramatic Entrance

I rose to my feet, stared at him for some seconds in utter amazement, and then it appears that I must have fainted for the first and the last time in my life. . . . "My dear Watson," said the well-remembered voice, "I owe you a thousand apologies. . . . I have given you a serious shock by my unnecessarily dramatic reappearance."

—"The Empty House"

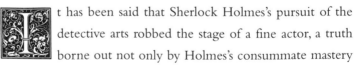 t has been said that Sherlock Holmes's pursuit of the detective arts robbed the stage of a fine actor, a truth borne out not only by Holmes's consummate mastery of disguise but also by his talent for making dramatic entrances, exits, and revelations. Surely his reputation as history's greatest detective was cemented in part thanks to this ability, and the indelible impression his surprising methods made upon his—*what*

else to call them?—audiences. For though you might possess all of Holmes's stupendous powers of deduction and analysis, without his flair for the dramatic, your name will never be known beyond the walls of the local courthouse or police precinct.

• **Shed a disguise suddenly.** Few things are more shocking than watching one person become another, which is exactly the effect produced when Sherlock Holmes breaks character while in disguise. In *The Sign of the Four,* for example, Watson and another man are surprised when a decrepit seaman comes calling at the Baker Street apartment, only to begin speaking in Holmes's voice: "We both started in our chairs . . .'Holmes!' I exclaimed. . . . 'But where is the old man?' 'Here is the old man,' said he, holding out a heap of white hair."

• **Appear where you are least expected.** In *The Hound of the Baskervilles,* Watson is led to believe he is alone while investigating Sir Henry Baskerville's bizarre death on England's West Country moors while Holmes attends to other matters in distant London. The doctor has tracked a mysterious and possibly dangerous man to an ancient stone house on the moors and is waiting for him to return, pistol at the ready, when "a well-known voice" sounds outside the door: "It is a lovely evening, dear Watson." So surprised is

"SHED YOUR DISGUISE SUDDENLY. FEW THINGS ARE MORE
SHOCKING THAN WATCHING ONE PERSON BECOME ANOTHER."

Watson that he finds himself temporarily unable to breathe, and it is a moment or two before his senses return: "Holmes," he cries, shaken. "Holmes!"

• **Reveal key evidence in an unusual manner.** "The Naval Treaty" case hinges upon a missing document of great importance, upon which rests the entire reputation and career of a young man named Percy Phelps. Naturally, Holmes finds the treaty and returns it to the lad—but rather than simply handing it to him, Holmes delivers it under the lid of a food tray supposed to contain the man's breakfast. "Phelps raised the cover, and as he did so he uttered a scream . . . and then danced madly about the room, passing [the treaty] to his bosom and shrieking out in his delight. Then he fell back into an arm-chair so limp and exhausted with his own emotions that we had to pour brandy down his throat to keep him from fainting. 'There, there!' said Holmes, soothing, patting him upon the shoulder. 'It was too bad to spring it on you like this, but Watson here will tell you that I never can resist a touch of the dramatic.'"

• **Employ alarming props.** The first time Holmes appears in "The Adventure of the Black Peter," he strides into the Baker Street apartment with "a huge barbed-headed spear tucked like an umbrella under his arm. 'Good gracious, Holmes!'" Watson cries. "'You don't mean to say that you have been walking about London with that thing?'"

• **Disguise yourself as a decoy of yourself.** Though it's no easy feat to pull off, Holmes employed this technique to spectacular effect in "The Mazarin Stone." Holmes agrees to leave the room in which he's been negotiating with two criminals for the return of the precious Mazarin stone, but instead secretly takes the place of a wax replica of himself that's been lurking in the corner. When the thieves, thinking they're alone, produce the stone, the "replica" of Holmes springs to life and grabs it. The villains' utter amazement is a testament to Holmes's success: "The Count's bewilderment overmastered his rage and fear. 'But how the deuce—?' he gasped."

• **Stage a collapse.** "We have had some dramatic entrances and exits upon our small stage at Baker Street," writes Watson in "The Priory School," "but I cannot recollect anything more sudden and startling than the first appearance of Thorneycroft Huxtable, M.A., Ph.D., etc." A most self-possessed and pompous-looking man had come to call and surprised all present when "his first action after the door had closed behind him was to stagger against the table, whence he slipped down upon the floor, and there was that majestic figure prostrate and insensible upon our bearskin hearthrug." Should you ever have cause to fake an illness, this is an excellent way to commence your performance.

The Real Sherlock Holmes

I thought of my old teacher Joe Bell, of his eagle face, of his curious ways, of his eerie trick of spotting details. If he were a detective he would surely reduce this fascinating but unorganized business to something nearer an exact science.

—Arthur Conan Doyle, from his autobiography

here is an entire branch of Sherlockian scholarship that trades upon the playful assumption that Sherlock Holmes and Dr. Watson were real people, and that the well-loved Holmes mysteries are not fiction at all but actual events, expertly documented by Watson and published under the name of his friend and literary agent, Arthur Conan Doyle. "The Great Game," as these speculative works of scholarship are called, are generally regarded as an ambitious and amusing distraction, but there may be at least a kernel of truth to them: If one were to ask Sir Arthur whether or not Sherlock Holmes was real, his answer may well have been in the affirmative.

The "real" Sherlock Holmes was a doctor and lecturer named Joseph Bell, under whom Conan Doyle studied while in medical school and upon whom he would later base his most famous character. Bell wasn't interested in crime, of course, but he was a detective of medicine whose impressive observations and deductions inspired his students and colleagues, Conan Doyle especially. In an 1892 letter to his former mentor, Conan Doyle wrote: "I do not think that [Holmes's] analytical work is in the least an exaggeration of some effects which I have seen you produce in the out-patient ward. Round the centre of deduction and inference and observation which I have heard you inculcate, I have tried to build up a man who pushed the thing as far as it would go—further occasionally."

Anecdotes that illustrate Dr. Bell's legendary skills of observation and deduction are plentiful, and a few seem to mirror Holmes's methods almost exactly. One recalls the doctor's uncanny ability to deduce a patient's occupation, history, and hometown within moments of first meeting. After having performed this medical parlor trick on a female patient for the benefit of his students, Bell explains how he did it:

You see, gentlemen, when she said good morning to me I noted her Fife accent, and, as you know, the nearest town in Fife is Burntisland. You noticed the red clay on the edges of the soles of her shoes, and the only such clay within 20 miles of Edinburgh is in the Botanic Gardens. Inverleith Row borders the gardens and is her nearest way here from Leith. You observed that the coat she carried over her arm is too big for the child who is with her, and therefore she set out from home with two children. Finally she has a dermatitis on the finger of the right hand which is peculiar to workers in the linoleum factory in Burntisland.

But the astute doctor didn't limit his observations to the clinic. Another story puts Bell in a tearoom at a Scottish golf resort, where he overhears two elderly golfers arguing about the location of a village near the English town of Blackheath. Bell interjects, suggesting they put the question to a fourth man in the room, who is finally able to provide the answer. After the old men leave, the fourth man asks Bell, "What led you to refer them to me, a stranger?" Bell replies, "Well, I saw you this morning pivoting on your left foot on the golf course. That is a fault of those who learned their golf in boyhood. I heard you speak and knew you were English. Blackheath was about the only place in England where golf could be learned forty years ago, and I thought it probable you would know the neighborhood."

Bell was proud of—if somewhat modest about—his connection to Sherlock Holmes and deflected flattering comparisons by claiming that Conan Doyle's "imaginative genius" had made "a great deal out of very little." But the author would have none of it, insisting in his autobiography that "it is all very well to say that a man is clever, but the reader wants to see examples of it—such examples as Bell gave us every day in the wards."

How to Sniff Out a Hoax

"I thought over the matter all day, and by evening I was in low spirits again; for I had quite persuaded myself that the whole affair must be some great hoax or fraud, though what its object might be I could not imagine."

—"The Adventure of the Red-Headed League"

t least three times in his career Sherlock Holmes was tasked to unravel an elaborate hoax, and by employing some of the methods detailed here as well as his renowned deductive ability, the great detective never failed to do so. Should you suspect that a fraud is being perpetrated, these are means with which to identify the hallmarks of a confidence man and his deceptions.

- **If a deal seems too good to be true, be suspicious.** In each of the hoaxes Holmes foiled, the nature of the bait was identical: a rich, seemingly one-sided deal offered to a perfect stranger in which it wasn't clear what the offering party stood to gain. In "The Red-Headed League," for instance, a man is well compensated for a useless task—copying the encyclopedia *Britannica*—simply because of his ruddy hair. Holmes's "Three Garridebs" adventure concerns an elderly gentleman promised vast sums by a remote benefactor, which he has done nothing to deserve other than possessing an unusual surname (the titular "Garridebs"). Finally, a young clerk named Pycroft in "The Stockbroker's Clerk" is offered a rich position for which he is surely not qualified: a job managing an international corporation.

- **Identify contradictions or discrepancies in the story.** Every con man has a story—often an elaborate one—that sounds credible on the surface. But the devil is in the details, of which a criminal will provide many in order to appear convincing. The con man assumes both an identity and a milieu that is likely not native to him, and the more he explains himself, the more he is likely to contradict his own story, or to make some error in jargon. Be on the look-out for such missteps.

• **Look for out-of-character details.** Con men will put on airs to gain your confidence, purporting to be of a higher station in society than they really are. In "The Three Garridebs," Holmes notices that a man who claims to be a wealthy lawyer recently arrived from America is wearing "an English coat frayed at the elbow and trousers bagged at the knee with a year's wear." In "The Stockbroker's Clerk," young Pycroft is suspicious when the offices of the "international corporation" to which he had supposedly been hired turn out to be nothing more than "dusty little rooms, uncarpeted and uncurtained," the employer himself sporting a rotten tooth "very badly stuffed with gold." Low-class mannerisms of speech can also be revealing, as can misspellings and grammatical errors in written correspondence.

• **Question the suspected con man in a friendly manner.** You may not glean additional clues from a few easygoing questions, but you will soon discover how he reacts to them. If he has nothing to hide, his demeanor will be relaxed, but if he grows irritable or nervous—or seems to resent overmuch the involvement of a detective—you have further cause to be suspicious.

• **Perform a background check.** Because con men and hoaxsters tend to operate under assumed names, it's often difficult to discover their true identity. But as you close your net around them, it's vital to know whether you're dealing with a petty criminal or a sociopathic murderer who wouldn't hesitate to add you to his tally of victims. In "The Three Garridebs," Holmes tracks down the identity of con man "Killer Evans" by cross-referencing personal details such as the man's height, age, race, and probable place of birth with police records. This is a sound method, for it's likely that a veteran con man has had prior run-ins with the law.

• **Do what they ask of you.** The hoaxster will inevitably ask some small thing of you: that you follow him somewhere, leaving some crucial possession unguarded, or give him access to your personal accounts. If you're certain of his intent to defraud, the best way to snare the rogue is to catch him in the act. In "The Red-Headed League," Holmes deduces that the hoax's ruddy-haired target is being paid to copy the encyclopedia at an office across town in order to lure him away from his pawnbrokership for several hours each day, so that a team of thieves might burrow under his floor and into an adjacent bank vault. Only by allowing the thieves to make an attempt on the vault could they be caught, and their guilt inexorably proven.

Secret Societies and the Criminal Underworld

"To the scientific student of the higher criminal world no capital in Europe offered the advantages which London then possessed."

—Sherlock Holmes, "The Norwood Builder"

t the beginning of Queen Victoria's reign, London was a festering hotbed of criminality. Police in 1867 estimated that no fewer than 100,000 of its citizens earned their living by thievery, and many organized themselves into thriving gangs of pickpockets, whores, burglars, and counterfeiters. The successful ones lived like gentlemen, kept servants, and occasionally graduated from crime to capitalist enterprise. But the public outcry for better policing eventually yielded results, and as the nineteenth century drew to a close Scotland Yard had dramatically reduced crime in London. Perhaps as a result, Sherlock Holmes was rarely tasked to investigate common street crime, but hunted malefactors of a more devious nature. To the extent that the worst of them were driven underground, it's no surprise that Holmes encountered some of the most notorious secret societies of his time.

• **The Mafia.** By 1900, the Mafia controlled much of Sicily's economy but lacked a significant toehold in London. In the "Red Circle" adventure, Holmes runs across a young Italian couple who have betrayed the Mafia and are seeking refuge from a vicious hit man. "The Three Napoleons" also features a cadre of Mafia-connected villains, one of which Holmes calls "the greatest cut-throat in London." He goes on to explain that the Mafia "is a secret political society, enforcing its decrees by murder," a fact that would not have been as widely known to Conan Doyle's readers as it is to readers today. At that time, the Mafia was only just beginning to emerge as a force to be reckoned with in the Italian neighborhoods of American cities; previously *Mafioso* had been endemic only to Sicily. (Similar criminal organizations, including the Camorra in Naples, operated in other parts of Italy. In American parlance, however, *Mafia* has become a catch-all.)

• **The Molly Maguires.** Much of the late Holmes novel *The Valley of Fear* (1914) was based on the murderous doings of an Irish criminal organization called the Molly Maguires, although in *Valley* they're known as the "Scowrers." Active in the coal fields of western Pennsylvania from approximately the end of the Civil War until a series of spectacular arrests and trials broke them in 1876–78, the Mollies were a fraternity of aggrieved immigrant miners from Ireland. Forced to work in deplorable conditions and live in desperate poverty, with no one to protect them and anti-Irish anti-union policies the norm, they organized themselves and resisted their oppressors through terrorist acts. Sir Arthur's "Scowrers" and the real Mollies shared secret signals, passwords, and rites, though his wholly unsympathetic perspective ("A gang of murderers, are they not?" asks one character) isn't shared by all historians. The Mollies' twenty-year campaign of murder, fear, and intimidation was, if not justified by, then certainly provoked by the extreme injustices visited upon Irish miners and their families, and some argue that the Pinkerton detectives (and perhaps by fictional extension, Sherlock Holmes) were little more than strike-breakers acting in the interest of industrialist railroad magnates.

• **The Ku Klux Klan.** "The Adventure of the Five Orange Pips" concerns an Englishman who owned a plantation in

the American South and fought in the Confederate Army
before returning to England in 1869. Nearly two decades
later, the man's nephew engages the services of Sherlock
Holmes because his uncle has died mysteriously, not long
after receiving an envelope marked "K.K.K." and containing
five orange seeds (or pips). Holmes deduces that the pips are
a warning and the initials are not those of an individual but
of an organization: "'Have you never—' inquires Sherlock
Holmes, bending forward and sinking his voice—'have you
never heard of the Ku Klux Klan?'" Watson had not. Holmes
reads to him from an encyclopedia:

> *Ku Klux Klan A name derived from a fanciful resem-*
> *blance to the sound produced by cocking a rifle. This*
> *terrible secret society was formed by some ex-Confederate*
> *soldiers in the Southern States after the Civil War, and*
> *it rapidly formed local branches in different parts of the*
> *country, notably in Tennessee, Louisiana, the Carolinas,*
> *Georgia, and Florida. Its power was used for political*
> *purposes, principally for the terrorizing of [new] negro*
> *voters, and the murdering and driving from the country*
> *of those who were opposed to its views.*

The best known of several such terrorist organizations in the

South after the Civil War (the Knights of the White Camellia and the Southern Cross were others), the Klan meant to wrest away what little power Reconstruction had granted to Southern blacks. It aimed to solidify white power and effectively continue the Confederacy in an underground fashion, by threats, violence, and murder. It was officially disbanded in 1869, the same year Holmes's client's uncle left his plantation to return to England. In a fanciful play upon historical events, Holmes deduces that the reason the uncle had fled America was the same reason he was being hunted by the K.K.K.: He had betrayed them and stolen a great number of incriminating documents from the organization's leadership. (Though the real K.K.K. officially disbanded itself in 1869, many local chapters continued to sew havoc in a less formalized capacity; the organization experienced a resurgence after the 1915 release of D. W. Griffith's influential film *Birth of a Nation*, which glorified the original Klan.)

Spiritualism and the Occult

*"This agency stands flat-footed upon the ground,
and there it must remain. The world is big enough
for us. No ghosts need apply."*

—Sherlock Holmes, "The Sussex Vampire"

 ver the committed rationalist, Sherlock Holmes takes a hard line when it comes to the supernatural: "it's pure lunacy," he assures Watson in the "Sussex Vampire" case. "What have we to do with walking corpses who can only be held in the grave by stakes driven through their hearts?" (As it turns out, nothing: Holmes solves this case by deducing that a mother suspected of sucking her infant's blood was instead sucking poison from wounds made by the child's jealous brother.) Holmes's skepticism was proved correct in *The Hound of the Baskervilles* as well, when he revealed the supposed "Hell-hound" to be nothing more than an angry dog doused with glowing phosphorous.

But the detective's attitude toward all things paranormal did not reflect that of his more credulous creator, Arthur Conan Doyle. Sir Arthur attended séances and dabbled in psychic studies from the time he wrote the first Holmes stories, but it wasn't until the devastating Great War drew to a close, taking with it the lives of many the author knew and cared about, that he committed himself to (and came out publicly in full-throated support of) a paranormal belief system known as spiritualism. Mediumship and psychic phenomena so consumed Conan Doyle's attention in his later life that he was compelled to write a comprehensive two-volume *History of Spiritualism* (1926), toured the world giving lectures to spread the parapsychological gospel, and devoted major portions of his autobiography (*Memories and Adventures*, 1924) to the espousal of Spiritualist principles. He also penned *Pheneas Speaks* (1927), the collected transcriptions of spirit messages supposedly received by his wife, Lady Doyle.

Inevitably, Doyle's beliefs found their way into his fiction, informing the plots of several occult short stories and the novel *The Parasite* (1894), about a woman who uses hypnosis to victimize people. Despite Sherlock Holmes's unshakable skepticism, there are even a few hints of the paranormal that leak into the utterly reasonable world of Baker Street. For instance, in "The Problem of Thor Bridge" Watson refers to a number of cases that Holmes was never able to solve, not because of any failure on the detective's part, but because they were, in Watson's words, "unfathomable." "Among these unfinished tales is that of Mr. James Phillimore, who, stepping back into his own house to get his umbrella, was never more seen in this world. No less remarkable is that of the cutter *Alicia*, which sailed one spring morning into a small patch of mist from where she never again emerged, nor was anything further ever heard of herself and her crew. A third case worthy of note is that of Isadora Persano, the well-known journalist and duellist, who was found stark staring mad with a match box in front of him which contained a remarkable worm said to be unknown to science." Watson never goes so far as to dub these mysteries "supernatural," but neither does he close the door on such a possibility.

Doyle's spiritualist proclivities have even prompted scholars to propose that he wrote Sherlock Holmes as a clandestine psychic. "How else to account for the intuitive brilliance which Holmes passed off as deduction?" one wrote. Taking the hypothesis a step further, the same critic suggests that Holmes's occasional cocaine binges might actually be "attempts to blot out the disturbing visions of a clairvoyant." A fascinating theory, certainly, but ultimately it's one more to be added to Holmes's "unsolved cases" file.

How to Deal with Friends and Relations

"[Holmes] loathed every form of society with his whole Bohemian soul."

—"A Scandal in Bohemia"

herlock Holmes was a man who seemed to require neither love nor companionship, who was as happy alone with his chemistry experiments and cocaine bottle as he was in the company of others. "Sometimes I found myself regarding him as . . . a brain without a heart," Watson writes, "as deficient in human sympathy as he was preeminent in intelligence." Of course, one cannot avoid having a family—in Holmes's case an elder brother, Mycroft, whom he admired in a limited way—and just the same, a great detective must cultivate a friendship or two. After all, without Watson, who would've publicized Holmes's exploits? Without publicity, who would've hired Holmes? One must tend to friendships and relations as to vegetables in a garden: nurture them lest they wither.

• **Keep them close . . . but not too close.** Holmes often finds himself in need of Watson's practical assistance, but rarely his confidence; for that, one might consider employing the services of a psychiatrist—as novelist and filmmaker Nicholas Meyer imagined Holmes did in *The Seven-Per-Cent Solution*—or choose another line of work. Noting Holmes's love of secrecy, Watson writes that the detective "left even his closest friend guessing as to what his exact plans might be. He pushed to an extreme the axiom that the only safe plotter was he who plotted alone. I was nearer him than anyone else, and yet I was always conscious of the gap between." As for Holmes's brother Mycroft, he played a major role in only three of Holmes's cases; if the detective had some other confidant, he never mentioned it.

• **Trust family before friends.** When Holmes fakes his death to escape his vanquished enemy's vengeful henchmen in "The Final Problem," he tells Watson nothing of it. For three years, the good doctor suffers the loss not only of his wife from consumption but of his closest friend as well— who in reality has been sightseeing in the Far East, biding his time for an eventual return to London. Holmes communicates only with his brother Mycroft, and despite occasional thoughts of Watson during his exile, he admits that in the end he didn't quite trust his old friend: "I feared lest your affectionate regard for me should tempt you to some indiscretion which would betray my secret," he says. Blood, it seemed to Holmes, was more reliable than friendship.

• **Defend them with your life.** Though Holmes rarely gives voice to his affection for Watson under normal circumstances, his feelings come into stark relief when Watson is in danger. In a touching moment from "The Three Garridebs," Holmes dotes on his friend after the doctor takes a bullet in the leg then turns to Watson's assailant like a mother bear defending its cub: "By the Lord, it is as well for you. If you had killed Watson, you would not have got out of this room alive!" Watson writes, "It was worth a wound—it was worth many wounds—to know the depth of loyalty and love which lay behind that cold mask . . . the one and only time I caught a glimpse of a great heart as well as of a great brain."

• **Stick by old friends, whatever their infirmities.** Sherlock Holmes wasn't a man who made friends easily, but neither did he dispose of them—though unemotional, Holmes was steadfast in his relationships. A classic example is that of Charlie Peace, one of the few friends besides Watson whom Holmes ever mentions by name: "My old friend Charlie Peace was a violin virtuoso," he says in "The Illustrious Client." Peace was many other things besides: a burglar, a murderer, an actor, and an inventor who never comes to call on his old friend Holmes, simply enough, because he was hanged for his many crimes two years before the detective took up his first case. Whatever else it says about Holmes that he would associate with such a villain, his refusal to renounce their friendship is a testament to his fidelity.

Mycroft Holmes, Sherlock's Smarter Sibling

"He has the tidiest and most orderly brain, with the greatest capacity for storing facts, of any man. . . living. All other men are specialists, but his specialism is omniscience."

—Sherlock Holmes of Mycroft, "The Bruce-Partington Plans"

 herlock Holmes was as unemotional as he was secretive, traits that may explain how Dr. Watson could have known him for seven years before learning that

Holmes had an older brother in London named Mycroft. "I had come to believe that he was an orphan with no relatives living," Watson writes in "The Greek Interpreter," "but one day, to my very great surprise, he began to talk to me about his brother." Even more surprising are Holmes's assertions that Mycroft is unquestionably his intellectual superior, possessing an "extraordinary faculty for figures" and "better powers of observation than I." "Again and again I have taken a problem to him," Holmes says, "and have received an explanation which has afterwards proved to be the correct one." Despite his great abilities, however, Mycroft rarely lends any meaningful aid to his brother and appears in only three stories.

The reason, Holmes explains, is that not only has Mycroft "no energy" and "no ambitions of any kind," but that his brilliant mind is "absolutely incapable of working out the practical points which must be gone into before a case could be laid before a judge or jury." Watson's description of Mycroft in "The Greek Interpreter," as a slothful man with a powerful brain, seems to support Holmes's assertions: He is "heavily built and massive," Watson writes, with an "unwieldy frame" but "a head so masterful in its brow . . . that after the first glance one forgot the gross body and remembered only the dominant mind." With a brotherly mix of respect and disdain, Sherlock sums up the problem even more succinctly: "If the art of the detective began and ended

in reasoning from an armchair, my brother would be the greatest criminal agent that ever lived."

But a few years later, during the case of the "Bruce-Partington Plans," Holmes paints a more nuanced portrait of Mycroft. It seems that his earlier description of his brother's job—"he audits the books in some of the government departments"—was an understatement made for the sake of national security. "One has to be discreet when one talks of high matters of state," Holmes tells Watson mysteriously. "You are right in thinking that he is under the British government. You would also be right in a sense if you said that occasionally he IS the British government," Holmes says, adding that he's "the most indispensable man in the country."

Mycroft's mind is so orderly, Holmes elaborates, that the British government uses it as the "central exchange, the clearinghouse" for sensitive information from "every department." His function is not unlike that of a modern-day computer. "Suppose that a minister needs information as to a point which involves the Navy, India, Canada, and the bimetallic question," Holmes says. "He could get his separate advices from various departments upon each, but only Mycroft can focus them all, and say offhand how each factor would affect the other. They began by using him as a short-cut, a convenience; now he has made himself an essential. In that great brain of his everything is pigeon-holed and can be handed out in an instant."

And yet, like a computer, Mycroft is a man most firmly—and strangely—set in his ways. "I extremely dislike altering my habits," he grumbles in "The Bruce-Partington Plans," and Holmes concurs: His brother is as likely to change his routine as "a planet . . . [to] leave its orbit." Mycroft's rigid schedule is strictly divided between work and leisure time spent at the "Diogenes Club"— from exactly "quarter to five to twenty to eight" each day, Holmes says. Founded by Mycroft himself, the Diogenes Club is described by Holmes as "one of the queerest" in London, founded for men who, "some from shyness, some from misanthropy, . . . [are] the most unsociable and unclubable men in town." Inside, members peruse "the latest periodicals" alone, in total silence, and "no member is allowed to take the least notice of any other one." Proof positive, at last, that there were Londoners who loathed society more than Sherlock Holmes himself.

How to Manage Children

*"I have frequently gained my first real insight into
the character of parents by studying their children."*
—Sherlock Holmes, "The Copper Beeches"

t follows that someone as profoundly disinterested in
women as Holmes should loathe the presence of children, but such was not entirely the case: If not lovable
he found them at least useful, and several times he employed them
in the solution of a case. His knowledge extended even beyond
his scruffy band of preadolescent assistants known as the "Baker
Street Irregulars" to the nature of children in general, whom he
regarded as a valuable storehouse of information about their parents. Inasmuch as a detective's area of study is human nature, you
should be familiar with children, and how to handle them.

- **Be firm, but fair.** In "The Adventure of Shoscombe Old
Place," Watson describes a man as wearing "the firm, austere

"IN A CROWDED METROPOLIS LIKE LONDON, CHILDREN
MAKE PERFECT SPIES."

expression which is only seen upon those who have to control horses or boys." Firm austerity may be a fair description of the way in which Holmes handles his Baker Street boys as well. When a dozen of them clatter into his apartment in *The Sign of the Four*, he sternly reminds them that he "cannot have the house invaded in this way" yet proceeds to give them instructions, underground fare, and even an advance on their pay. In turn, they pay him respect likely given to no other adult: "There was some show of discipline among them," Watson reports, "for they instantly drew up in line and stood facing us with expectant faces."

• **Make them your eyes and ears.** In a crowded metropolis like London, Holmes explains, children make perfect spies: "They can go everywhere, see everything, overhear every one." This is just how he uses his dozen or so "irregulars," the street urchins who in *The Sign of the Four* are sent to find a steamship afloat somewhere on the Thames, and later employed by Holmes as sentries and tails.

• **Don't be afraid to give them responsibility.** They may be small, but some children are capable in a way that belies their diminutive stature, especially if they are given the chance to impress celebrated detective Sherlock Holmes. In

The Hound of the Baskervilles, Holmes depends heavily on a young man of fourteen named Cartwright: First the detective asks him to search every wastepaper basket in twenty-three London hotels—a not inconsiderable task—and later in the tale, when Holmes is hiding out on the moors of the West Country, the boy becomes the detective's sole provider of food, clothing, and information. "What does man want more?" Holmes later asks a bemused Watson. "He has given me an extra pair of eyes upon a very active pair of feet, and both have been invaluable."

• **Learn to read their inherited characteristics.** In the "Copper Beeches" case, Holmes says, "I was able, by watching the mind of the child, to form a deduction as to the criminal habits of the very smug and respectable father." That the six-year-old boy in question is fantastically cruel to small animals and, according to his governess, spends every day "in an alternation between fits of passion and gloomy intervals of sulking" is a point that Holmes judges to be of extreme importance. When it's finally revealed that the father has been holding his wayward daughter captive in a disused wing of his house, Holmes is not at all surprised; he has long since deduced the father's true nature from that of his cruel child.

Be Aware

Don't assume that all children can be trusted. A child with reason to hurt you will do so without hesitation and without the troublesome moral compunction of a like-minded adult. After all, it was an innocent-looking Swiss lad who betrayed Holmes and Watson in "The Final Problem," luring Watson away with a bogus letter and leaving Holmes to face his death (or so Watson thought) at the hands of his nemesis, Moriarty.

Common Misconceptions About Sherlock Holmes

or Sherlock Holmes, being one of the world's most recognizable characters means that a great many more people know who he is—or think they do—than have actually read his stories. Add to this the fact that innumerable film, television, theatrical, and radio adaptations of the Holmes stories have taken certain liberties with Conan Doyle's source material, and it seems inevitable that misconceptions about the detective should become ingrained in the popular imagination. This is an attempt to correct some of the most common of these misconceptions.

- **Holmes often exclaims "Elementary, my dear Watson!"** Although Holmes makes frequent use of the word "elementary," in Conan Doyle's stories he never utters the phrase so often attributed to him. (He does, however, say "*Exactly*, my dear Watson" on numerous occasions.) The misattributed saying first appeared in P. G. Wodehouse's novel *Psmith, Journalist* (1915): "'Elementary, my dear Watson, elementary,' murmured Psmith."

• **Holmes wears a deerstalker hat.** In "Silver Blaze," Watson describes Holmes as wearing an "ear-flapped traveling cap," which illustrator Sydney Paget interpreted to be a deerstalker hat. Famously double brimmed, the deerstalker is an outdoorsman's hat, designed to protect both the face and the back of the neck from sun exposure. You may be certain, however, that an urbane fashion-conscious gentleman such as Holmes would never be caught wearing a hunting cap in the city—a dire faux pas indeed. But Paget drew the detective wearing the deerstalker on seven separate occasions, effectively cementing it onto Holmes's head for all time.

• **Holmes was a handsome devil.** On the contrary, Conan Doyle had imagined the detective as having "a thin, razor-like face, with a great hawk's-bill of a nose, and two small eyes set close together." If that doesn't sound quite like the description of a matinee idol, illustrator Sydney Paget didn't think so either, and instead he used his strikingly handsome brother Walter as a model. Conan Doyle never took Paget to task over the matter, though. "Perhaps," the writer admitted, "from the point of view of my lady readers it was just as well."

• **Holmes used a curved calabash-style pipe.** The item most closely associated with the Holmes character is certainly his pipe, and though he undoubtedly spends a great deal of time smoking one in Conan Doyle's stories, the author never offers a clear description of it. Holmes's use of a curved, S-shaped pipe was originated by stage actor William Gillette around the turn of the last century; Gillette chose it because the drooping shape wouldn't interfere with his famous profile.

• **Holmes never laughed and rarely smiled.** The detective's reputation as a cold and sober calculating machine fed the myth that the man was mirthless—a myth propagated even in the stories themselves. In "The Mazarin Stone," an unnamed narrator writes that "Holmes seldom laughed, but he got as near it as his old friend Watson could remember." But Holmesian scholar Edward S. Lauterbach has proved otherwise by composing the following table (abridged):

Frequency Table Showing the Number and Kind of Responses Sherlock Holmes Made to Humorous Situations and Comments in His 60 Recorded Adventures.

Smile	103	Delight	7
Laugh	65	Twinkle	7
Chuckle	31	Miscellaneous	19

Throughout the twentieth century, countless film and television productions have brought Sidney Paget's rich illustrations to life, so it's no wonder most readers imagine Sherlock Holmes looking something like the man shown here (on the left). But Doyle's physical descriptions, along with Holmes' actions throughout the canon, suggest a visage that is much closer to the man shown on the right.

How to Deal with Women

"I would not tell them too much," said Holmes.
"Women are never to be entirely trusted — not the
best of them."
—*The Sign of the Four*

hough Sherlock Holmes could admire the beauty of a handsome woman as well as any gentleman, he had no use for them romantically. Practical to the point of being cold, he sneers at the news of Dr. Watson's engagement in *The Sign of the Four*, remarking that "love is an emotional thing, and whatever is emotional is opposed to that true cold reason which I place above all things. I should never marry myself, lest I bias my judgment." Whether or not you agree that romance is anathema to reason, the budding detective would do well to study Holmes's professional approach to the fairer sex, which helped steer many a case to its successful conclusion.

• **Always be a gentleman.** Although Holmes often expressed his distrust (and occasionally even his dislike) of women, Watson writes of his "remarkable gentleness and courtesy" when dealing with them and notes with some amazement that his "ingratiating" manner made it easy for women to confide in him. Certainly his ability to turn on the charm made the questioning of female witnesses easier, as it did in "The Adventure of the Golden Pince Nez," in which Holmes is found chatting with a suspect's housekeeper "as if he had known her for years" only minutes after meeting for the first time.

• **Take care when attempting to deduce their motives.** Holmes believed that although the motives of male criminals are usually uncomplicated—money, power, and revenge being paramount among them—the motives of women are "inscrutable . . . their most trivial action may mean volumes, or their most extraordinary conduct may depend upon a hairpin." In "The Problem of Thor Bridge," a bereaved American tycoon agrees with Holmes, hypothesizing that "women lead an inward life and may do things beyond the judgment of men." Add to that Holmes's conviction that women are "naturally secretive" and you have a veritable deductive minefield; the female mind as an enigma that reason alone cannot pene-

trate. In your own investigations, therefore, never allow your-self to assume you understand their motives.

• **Use their emotions to your advantage.** It may seem callous, but women's easily manipulated emotions—to the extent that they cloud their bearer's better judgment—can be useful to the cunning detective. A prime example is the case of "Charles Augustus Milverton," in which Holmes becomes engaged to the titular man's housemaid while disguised as a plumber, solely to gain information about her employer. Despite Watson's moral objections—"Surely you have gone too far?" he insists—Holmes maintains the cruel ruse until the case is solved and Milverton, a usurer and blackmailer of the worst sort, is killed. The successful end, to Holmes's mind at least, justified the rather unpleasant means.

• **Underestimate them at your peril.** One of the few failures of Holmes's career came at the hands of an American opera singer named Irene Adler. It's tempting to underestimate the cunning of a woman described as "the daintiest thing under a bonnet," and Holmes did so at his peril. In an attempt to steal a damaging photograph of Miss Adler and Holmes's client, the King of Bohemia, Holmes dons a disguise to gain her confidence and infiltrate her home. But she sees through the master detective's costume—one of the few persons ever to do so—and flees with the photograph before Holmes has a chance to snatch it. Thus does "A Scandal in Bohemia" end on an unusual down note: "And that was how a great scandal threatened to affect the kingdom of Bohemia, and how the best plans of Mr. Sherlock Holmes were beaten by a woman's wit. He used to make merry over the cleverness of women, but I have not heard him do it of late."

• **Beware a woman scorned.** More than one tragedy in the annals of Holmes's career was precipitated by a jealous woman; perhaps the detective's exposure to such misfortunes played a role in his personal rejection of romantic love. In "The Problem of Thor Bridge," for example, a husband's affection for his children's governess makes his wife "crazy with hatred" and apparently provokes her suicide, which she stages to look like a murder committed by the despised governess. The probable killer in "The Musgrave Ritual" is a maid named Rachel Howells, who is suspected in the death of her unfaithful lover, though conclusive proof is unavailable. "The Illustrious Client" features a cad who has made a sport of seducing women and then destroying them; one such victim is described as having "an intensity of hatred in her . . . blazing eyes such as women seldom and man never can attain."

How to Keep Your Mind Sharp

A long series of sterile weeks lay behind us, and here at last there was a fitting object for those remarkable powers which, like all special gifts, become irksome to their owner when they are not in use. That razor brain blunted and rusted with inaction.

—The Valley of Fear

 am a brain, Watson," Holmes famously quipped in "The Mazarin Stone." "The rest of me is mere appendix." It may sound like an exaggeration, but in one sense it was not. However much Holmes may have benefited from his expertise in self-defense or similar applications of the physical self, the primary instrument of his trade was his mind. For it was only by his powers of logical analysis and deduction that he could succeed where detectives before him had failed. Thus, in times of inaction or crisis it was crucial he find ways to keep his instrument sharp. Before undertaking Holmes's techniques for yourself, be aware that many of them have no positive effect on the body—some even render a deleterious effect—but such was not his priority.

- **Starve yourself.** Though Watson often nagged him to eat, Holmes rarely took food while working on a problem, and during especially taxing cases he sometimes went for days without a meal. "The faculties become refined when you starve them," he once explained to Watson. "As a doctor . . . you must admit that what your digestion gains in the way of blood supply is so much lost to the brain."

- **Smoke copiously.** Just because you refuse food while deep in thought doesn't mean you must live like an ascetic. Tobacco was the first thing Holmes reached for when puzzling over a problem: "Holmes had pushed away his untasted breakfast and lit the unsavoury pipe which was the companion of his deepest meditations," Watson writes in *The Valley of Fear.* While working on the "Mazarin Stone" case, Holmes humbly begs Watson not "to despise my pipe and my lamentable tobacco" because "it has to take the place of food these days." We learn still more of his habits while Holmes is contemplating the outlandish "Red-Headed League" mystery, so difficult he deems it "a three-pipe problem."

• **Ignore that which is unimportant.** Just because there are an endless number of things to be learned about the universe, Holmes proposes in *A Study in Scarlet*, doesn't mean one should try to learn them all—quite the opposite, in fact. When Watson is dumbstruck that his brilliant friend doesn't know the composition of Earth's solar system, Holmes lays out the following theory: "I consider that a man's brain originally is like a little empty attic, and you have to stock it with such furniture as you choose. A fool takes in all the lumber of every sort that he comes across, so that the knowledge which might be useful to his gets crowded out . . . it is of the highest importance, therefore, not to have useless facts elbowing out the useful ones."

• **Always keep your mind occupied.** "To let the brain work without sufficient material is like racing an engine," Holmes says in "The Devil's Foot." "It racks itself to pieces." When there is no case at hand—and sometimes even when there is—Holmes turns his attention to chemistry experiments, to his violin (the introspective work of German composers is best for the mind, he claimed), or, in extreme cases, to cocaine. Watson defends his friend's taste for the latter thusly: "He only turned to the drug as a protest against the monotony of existence when cases were scanty and the papers uninteresting." Holmes himself provides a somewhat less apologetic explanation: "I suppose that its influence is physically a bad one. I find it, however, so transcendently stimulating and clarifying to the mind that its secondary action is a matter of small moment."

Sherlock Holmes and Music

Holmes was an enthusiastic musician, being himself not only a very capable performer of no ordinary merit.

—"The Red-Headed League"

olmes's passion for music was second only to his passion for detective work, and he brought the same obsessive intensity and depth of knowledge to bear upon both pursuits. Had he not applied his talents to the apprehension of criminals and deduction of misdeeds, surely he would have found his calling as a professional violinist, or at the very least a peerless musicologist. As it was, the polymathic master detective somehow found the time and ambition to become an accomplished amateur musician and music scholar as well as a detective of world renown.

Above all, Holmes was a music lover. Music was his tonic: It calmed his nerves after periods of exertion and sharpened his keen mind during especially difficult cases. In the midst of the vexing "Red-Headed League" mystery, for instance, the detective insists that Watson accompany him to a concert by the renowned Spanish violinist Saraste. "All the afternoon he sat in the stalls wrapped in the most perfect happiness," Watson writes, "gently

waving his long, thin fingers in time to the music, while his gently smiling face and his languid, dreamy eyes were as unlike those of Holmes, the sleuth-hound, Holmes the relentless, keen-witted, ready-handed criminal agent, as it was possible to conceive."

It is almost as if Watson is describing a split personality, one in which Holmes the passionate music lover and Holmes the cold and calculating detecting machine require each other for the man to function. Revealingly, Watson asserts that Holmes "was never so truly formidable as when, for days on end, he had been lounging in his armchair amid his [musical] improvisations. . . . When I saw him that afternoon so enwrapped in the music at St. James's Hall I felt that an evil time might be coming upon those whom he had set himself to hunt down." Music, Watson claims here, is for Holmes a crucial kind of brain-fuel. Without music to feed him, we can assume, Holmes might never have become a detective of remarkable talents.

Holmes didn't merely enjoy music—he played it as well. But much like his association with other disciplines (chemistry, botany, geology), his talents were remarkable but unusual. Watson gives a full account:

That he could play pieces, and difficult pieces, I knew well, because at my request he has played me some of Mendelssohn's Lieder, and other favorites. When left to himself, however, he

would seldom produce any music or attempt any recognized air.
Leaning back in his arm-chair of an evening, he would close his
eyes and scrape carelessly at the fiddle which was thrown across
his knee. . . . I might have rebelled against these exasperating
solos had it not been that he usually terminated them by play-
ing in quick succession a whole series of my favorite airs as a
slight compensation for the trial upon my patience.

We know too that Holmes was a collector: He owned an
extremely rare and valuable Stradivarius violin that he boasted of
buying for a pittance from a merchant who had no clue of its
worth. In "The Mazarin Stone" Holmes has a gramophone,
which he uses to get the best of two thieves by tricking them into
believing that a recording of a violin solo is actually Holmes himself playing in another room.

As an alternative to his detective work, however, Holmes's
greatest professional promise—in the music world, at least—was
as a scholar. While still engaged in the mystery of "The Bruce-
Partington Plans," he finds time to lose himself in the writing of
"a monograph which he had undertaken upon the Polyphonic
Motets of Lassus." Apparently, this bit of scholarship was more
than just a trifle to distract himself from a taxing case; Watson later
mentions that Holmes's article on the Franco-Flemish composer
"has since been printed for private circulation, and is said by

experts to be the last word upon the subject." But his expertise doesn't end there. In "The Adventure of the Cardboard Box," he and Watson "sat for an hour over a bottle of claret while he told me anecdote after anecdote" about the Italian violin virtuoso Paganini, and in *A Study in Scarlet* Watson writes (with some exasperation) that Holmes "was in the best of spirits, and prattled away about Cremona fiddles, and the difference between a Stradivarius and an Amati."

It would be an exaggeration to say that Sherlock Holmes missed his true calling as a musician, for if he had given up his magnifying glass for a bow, the world of law enforcement would have missed him sorely. But Holmes loved music as he never loved a woman; music sustained him, and his great powers of detection veritably depended on it.

Opium Dens and Narcotics in the Victorian Era

"The division seems rather unfair," I remarked. "You have done all the work in this business. I get a wife out of it, Jones gets the credit, pray what remains for you?"
"For me," said Sherlock Holmes, "there still remains the cocaine bottle." And he stretched his long white hand up for it.
—The Sign of the Four

herlock Holmes was many things: peerless detective, logical genius, master of several natural sciences, and virtuoso violinist. He was also, by his own account, a drug addict. Holmes preferred a "seven-percent solution" of cocaine injected with a syringe, sometimes embarking on binges that left his "sinewy forearm and wrist all dotted and scarred with innumerable puncture-marks" as "for days on end he would lie upon the sofa . . . hardly uttering a word or moving a muscle from morning to night." In Holmes's defense, Watson characterizes his friend's habit as an "occasional" reaction to "the monotony of existence when cases were scanty and the papers uninteresting." But just a few years later, during the "Missing Three-Quarter" case, Watson admits the seriousness of Holmes's problem, revealing that he's only just begun to wean the detective "from that drug mania which had threatened once to check his remarkable career."

In an era when narcotics of all sorts were legal and freely available, when opiates were the active ingredient in countless over-the-counter patent medicines and heroin was marketed as a side-effect-free cough suppressant, Watson's recognition of cocaine's addictive powers was striking. Even the venerable *Encyclopedia Britannica*'s 1888 edition claims that addiction to narcotics "happens chiefly in individuals of weak will-power, who would just as easily become the victims of intoxicating drinks, and who are practically moral imbeciles, often addicted also to other forms of depravity."

It was an attitude toward drugs shared by many in the Victorian era. Shortly after German chemist Albert Niemann first isolated cocaine from coca leaves in 1859, it became a sensation in Europe and the United States. Hailed as a wonder drug, cocaine was widely consumed in the form of coca-fortified wine, and its fans included Queen Victoria, Sigmund Freud, and Pope Leo XIII, who endorsed it in advertisements and carried some coca-wine with him in a personal hip flask. Cocaine was especially popular with writers, artists, and intellectuals—Sherlock Holmes among them—many of whom credited the drug's stimulant

"THE REALITY OF LONDON'S OPIUM DENS DIDN'T
QUITE MATCH THEIR SENSATIONALIZED PORTRAYALS
BY CONAN DOYLE."

properties with their ability to work unforgiving hours.

By the turn of the twentieth century, however, the addictive powers of cocaine and opium were becoming undeniably clear, and the tide of public opinion was slowly but surely turning against them. Horrific depictions of opium dens in popular literature certainly played a role in this transformation, including Sherlock Holmes's famous turn as a disguised opium addict in "The Man with the Twisted Lip." Watson describes his descent into an East End opium den as one into Hell: "Through the gloom one could dimly catch a glimpse of bodies lying in strange fantastic poses, bowed shoulders, bent knees, heads thrown back, and chins pointing upward, with here and there a dark, lack-lustre eye turned upon the newcomer. Out of the black shadows there glimmered little red circles of light . . . as the burning poison waxed or waned in the bowls of the metal pipes." To Watson's utter surprise, Holmes the master of disguise is lurking in the den as well, though at first glance Watson only recognizes him as an "old man . . . bent with age, an opium pipe dangling down from between his knees, as though it had dropped in sheer lassitude from his fingers."

But the reality of London's opium dens didn't quite match their sensationalized portrayals by authors such as Conan Doyle, Charles Dickens, and Oscar Wilde. Rather than a slum teeming with dens and frequented by thousands of morally bankrupt

Chinese immigrants, the East End's Limehouse district never had more than a few hundred Chinese and about a half-dozen opium dens—if you could even call them that. On the whole, these "dens" were simply rooms where Chinese men gathered to smoke opium, gamble, and gossip; they were more like informal social clubs than dens of desperate iniquity (or as Holmes describes the den he visits in "Twisted Lip," "the vilest murder-trap on the whole riverside"). It's not known exactly how many Londoners slummed it in opium dens, but the general impression at the time was surely exaggerated; many more Victorians partook of and became addicted to opium in the form of laudanum—an alcoholic derivative so popular it was spoon-fed to teething infants—than by smoking it, a practice that suggested exotic danger simply because it was associated with the "alien" culture of Chinese immigrants.

How to Interact with Royalty

Holmes: "It is a little souvenir from the King of Bohemia in return for my assistance in the case of the Irene Adler papers."
Watson: "And the ring?"
Holmes: "It was from the reigning family of Holland, though the matter in which I served them was of such delicacy that I cannot confide it even to you."

—"A Scandal in Bohemia"

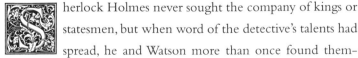herlock Holmes never sought the company of kings or statesmen, but when word of the detective's talents had spread, he and Watson more than once found themselves entertaining royalty in their modest rooms on Baker Street. But Holmes's temperament was unlike that of most commoners; he had neither the patience nor the humility to fawn or grovel before wealthy persons of noble birth, but neither could he treat

them with his typical brashness. His attitude was a careful balancing act, one that any detective aspiring to the pinnacle of his profession would do well to study.

- **Observe royal customs of courtesy.** Holmes rarely bows to anyone, save the occasional lady of noble bearing, but when the Lord St. Simon comes to call in "The Noble Bachelor," Holmes rolls out the proverbial red carpet, bowing and insisting his guest take the best seat. A few other proprieties one must observe while dealing with royalty: Address western European monarchs as "your majesty" and European heads of state, ambassadors, and high-ranking clergy members as "your excellency." Stand when a monarch enters the room, and wait until they have been seated to seat yourself. Most importantly, never turn your back on a royal. There are countless other such gestures, all of which you'll be thankful to know should you ever find yourself in the presence of the Queen.

- **Guard their secrets closely.** It is no small thing to have royal secrets entrusted to you, and to give them up is not only improper, it may be hazardous to your health. (Royal enemies are the worst kind!) Holmes refuses to divulge the details of royal cases even to Watson, and certainly not to other royal clients, as when Lord St. Simon presses for infor-

mation regarding the king of Scandinavia: "'You can understand,' Holmes replies suavely, 'that I extend to the affairs of
my other clients the same secrecy which I promise to you in
yours.'" What's more, lucrative clients tend to be referred by
other wealthy constituents, a revenue source easily jeopardized

by unfavorable word-of-mouth. A visit to Baker Street by the king of Bohemia is preceded by a note: "Your recent services to one of the royal houses of Europe have shown that you are one who may safely be trusted with matters which are of an importance which can hardly be exaggerated." One slip of the tongue, and Holmes's stream of deep-pocketed royal clients might very well have evaporated.

• **Don't hesitate to take their money.** When the king of Bohemia offers Holmes the equivalent of $100,000 in today's money for retrieving a single photograph, the detective accepts it without hesitation or comment. Wealthy clients like to think they can buy the best of anything—the service of great minds included—and it behooves neither you nor your client to shatter that illusion (or mention that yesterday, for example, you rendered services to a lowly fishmonger, pro bono, simply because you found the case intriguing). The Bohemian king later gifts Holmes with a gold snuffbox, the royal family of Holland presents him with an expensive ring, the French president awards a Legion of Honor medal, and it's implied that Queen Victoria herself bestows an emerald tie-pin upon the detective for his services in retrieving a set of sensitive documents in "The Bruce-Partington Plans." The only such honor Holmes is known to have refused was a knighthood in 1902 for, Watson writes mysteriously in "The Three Garridebs," "services which may perhaps some-day be described."

• **If they be clients, treat them as such.** Apart from the few added formalities you must heed when dealing with roy-als, it is in the best interest of all involved that you should otherwise treat them as you would any other client. A detec-tive struck dumb or giddy in the presence of nobility, or who becomes a cringing sycophant at the thought of the riches a wealthy client might bestow, is not a detective who is devot-ing the fullness of his faculties to the task at hand. As for Holmes, he was positively bored by gossipy reports of royal goings-on, and when congratulated by Watson on his deal-ings with nobles, he replied: "I assure you, Watson, without affectation, that the status of my client is a matter of less moment to me than the interest of his case."

How to Raise Bees

*My house is lonely. I, my old housekeeper, and my
bees have the estate all to ourselves.*
—Sherlock Holmes, "The Lion's Mane"

fter more than twenty years as a consulting detective,
in 1902 Sherlock Holmes chose to escape the gloom
of London and retire to a modest farmhouse in the
country. There he devoted himself to apiculture, the art of raising
bees—when he wasn't being called out of retirement on special
missions for the government, that is. One of the proudest achieve-
ments of his life—the "magnum opus of my later years," he calls
it—is a book he writes on the subject, *The Practical Handbook of
Bee Culture*. "Behold the fruit of pensive nights and laborious
days," he trumpets while showing off the volume to Watson,
"when I watched the little working gangs as once I watched the
criminal world of London." Follow the steps outlined below, and
you too can raise little winged gangs.

1. Choose a location. Like Holmes himself, bees are sensitive creatures and must be provided with just the right environment to thrive. They need moderate exposure to sunlight, protection from extreme temperatures, shelter from excessive wind, access to water, and a plentiful source of pollen with which they make honey, be it an orchard or a bountiful garden. In this way, the successful beekeeper must also be a successful gardener. (Interestingly, at the beginning of their careers together Watson noted that Holmes knew "nothing of practical gardening." We can only assume he developed a green thumb late in life.)

2. Build or purchase housing for your bees. The most commonly used beehive was developed in the mid-1800s, and its design hasn't changed a great deal since then. It consists of a multilayered box called a *super*, where the queen lays her eggs (up to 2,000 a day) and worker bees raise her brood, and a series of removable shelves placed about a quarter inch apart in which the bees store their honey. Another important feature is the queen excluder, a mesh screen that ensures the queen doesn't contaminate the honey by laying her eggs in it.

3. Gather supplies. Unless you're fond of stings, beekeeping is an equipment-intensive activity. Most apiculturists wear protective clothing made from thick light-colored material—thick so the bees' stingers can't penetrate and light-colored so that the creatures never confuse you with a honey-hungry brown bear. Thick gloves are a necessity, as is a hat with mosquito netting attached. A smoker will come in handy, for it drives the bees from the hive and makes them sluggish, creating a perfect opportunity to harvest the sticky, golden fruit of their labor.

4. Procure some bees. The best source is an experienced beekeeper or a commercial bee farmer. Bees can be sent by courier or through the post, but don't skimp on the postage; it's best not to leave them unattended for more than a few days.

5. Transfer the bees into their new hive. Give them about twenty-four hours to acclimate to their new surroundings before using your smoker to guide them from the box in which they arrived toward their new hive. You may want to place a sugar syrup solution in the hive to further encourage relocation. If the flowers aren't blooming at this time, you may need to feed them pollen supplements.

6. Harvest the honey. When the time comes to harvest the honey, scrape the honeycomb with a large spoon and collect the honey in a pail. Strain it through a sieve and then through muslin to separate the wax. Let it stand for several days until the air bubbles rise to the top, at which point the honey is ready for consumption.

APPENDIX

Briefly, the Life and Times of Sir Arthur Conan Doyle

STEEL TRUE
BLADE STRAIGHT
ARTHUR CONAN DOYLE
KNIGHT
PATRIOT, PHYSICIAN &
MAN OF LETTERS

—Sir Arthur Conan Doyle's epitaph

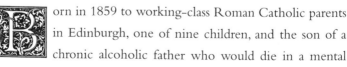 orn in 1859 to working–class Roman Catholic parents in Edinburgh, one of nine children, and the son of a chronic alcoholic father who would die in a mental institution, Conan Doyle hardly seemed destined for the fame and success he would one day achieve. But with his family's backing, young Arthur was sent to Jesuit prep schools and eventually

medical school at the University of Edinburgh, in the hope that he would escape poverty and make something of himself. He did, of course, and to a degree few could have anticipated.

It was at medical school that the teenaged Conan Doyle began to write stories and where he met Joseph Bell, a physician and lecturer whose keen mind and startling powers of observation would later inspire the Sherlock Holmes character. Not yet twenty years old, Conan Doyle succeeded in getting his first story published in a prominent Edinburgh magazine in 1879. A year later, another publisher recognized the budding author's talent and advised him to abandon medicine in favor of writing, but Conan Doyle was too

unsure of his literary talents—and too concerned about money—
to take that leap so early. Instead, he worked his way through
school, sending as much money home to his family as he could
manage. Jobs as a doctor on an arctic whaling ship in 1879 and a
West African steamer in 1880 whet his lifelong taste for adventure,
but almost killed him: He fell into the freezing sea from the former
so often that its captain called him "the Northern Diver," and he
nearly died of fever on the latter.

By age twenty-three Conan Doyle had established a modest
medical practice in the south of England, but a dearth of patients
allowed him plenty of time to write stories. It was then, lonely
and struggling, that he began to conceive of a detective named
Sherlock Holmes. Years later, Conan Doyle would explain that he
had long been a fan of detective stories—French writer Émile
Gaboriau "had rather attracted me with the neat dovetailing of
his plots, and Poe's masterful detective, M. Dupin, had from boyhood been one of my heroes"—but he was never satisfied with
the explanations of how these fictional detectives solved their
fantastic cases. Conan Doyle believed he could do better and
made his own detective a scientist whose deductions were always
transparently logical, if brilliantly wrought. Conan Doyle introduced Sherlock Holmes to the world in his first novel, 1887's *A
Study in Scarlet*, which earned him a mere £25 and attracted little interest. He followed it with a thriller, *The Mystery of Cloomber*

(1889), and two well-received novels of historical fiction. But if Conan Doyle hadn't revived Holmes in 1890's considerably more successful *The Sign of the Four*, both Holmes's career as a detective and Conan Doyle's as a writer might have ended there.

In 1891 he moved to London with his wife, Louise—the sister of a former patient—his daughter, and five novels already published, and finally decided to abandon medicine and devote his full attention to writing. "It was one of the great moments of exultation of my life," he later wrote. Courted by editors and agents, Conan Doyle published the first Sherlock Holmes short stories in *Strand* magazine, which immediately became a hot item at newsstands. Sherlock Holmes caught on like wildfire, and both the author and his celebrated detective quickly became famous.

Two years and twenty-four stories later, however, Conan Doyle had had quite enough of Sherlock Holmes—"If I have sometimes inclined to be weary of him it is because his character admits no light or shade," he explained in his autobiography—and led him to a watery grave in 1893's notorious "The Final Problem." Despite the outcry that arose from distraught Holmes fans the world over, Conan Doyle turned his back on the detective for nine years before writing *Hound of the Baskervilles* in 1902 and then bringing Holmes back for good in 1904, explaining that he had merely faked his death at Reichenbach Falls. (For more on Holmes's mysterious "hiatus," refer to page 115.)

The years that followed Holmes's famous demise were tragic for Conan Doyle as well: His wife contracted tuberculosis in
1893, and during thirteen long years, she sickened, became an
invalid, and finally succumbed to her illness. They traveled from
spa to spa, even living in arid Cairo for a time on the advice of
doctors, hoping her condition would improve. Instead it became
chronic, and as Louise fell deeper into what appeared to be a
death sentence, Conan Doyle began falling in love with another
woman, a beautiful opera singer named Jean Leckie. Caught
between his dying wife and his very much living infatuation, the
author's conscience was tortured for years. But he and Jean's relationship remained platonic until after Louise's death in 1906; they
married the following year.

In the meantime, Conan Doyle had been churning out a
succession of accomplished—but now largely forgotten—literary
works, from adventure novels and sports stories to a book set in
the Napoleonic era, *Uncle Bernac* (1897). When war broke out in
South Africa in 1898, Conan Doyle's ardent patriotism led him to
Cape Town, where he was too old to serve in the army but was
allowed to supervise a hospital. Afterward he penned an impas-
sioned defense of England's much-maligned involvement in the
conflict and ran for office as a candidate for Parliament. Though
he lost the election, his patriotism was unwavering; when the
Great War broke out in 1914, he was fifty-five years old but

attempted—unsuccessfully—to enlist anyway. He was knighted in 1902, some say for his support of the Boer War; devoted Holmes fans, on the other hand, claim he was honored for finally resuscitating Sherlock Holmes in *The Hound of the Baskervilles*. Some years later, the government approached Conan Doyle about heading up a propaganda division, and though he declined, Sherlock Holmes makes a comment in a late story that nevertheless reveals Conan Doyle's sympathy for the endeavor: "The press, Watson, is a most valuable institution, if you only know how to use it."

In addition to penning another thirty-two Holmes stories and one more Holmes novel (*The Valley of Fear*, 1915), Conan Doyle spent the remainder of his life producing an astonishing body of literary work. In 1912 he introduced his second most famous character, Professor Challenger, whom Conan Doyle would sustain through five novels (one of which, *The Lost World*, would inspire numerous adaptations, including the *Jurassic Park* franchise).

Conan Doyle's life after the Great War, however, was marked by tragedy and a search for greater meaning. Europe had endured the loss of millions of young men. His family suffered immensely: Close friends and relatives were butchered in the trenches, and both his son and his brother died of 'flu just months after the conflict ended. Sinking into a black depression, the long-agnostic author found that he couldn't live with the idea that so many he had loved had simply tumbled into the void, never to be heard from again. Conan Doyle had been dabbling in spiritualism, the religion of mediums and psychics, for twenty years, but it was at this dark time in his life that he devoted himself to it wholeheartedly. He visited mediums, attended séances, and would later say that "there is no physical sense I possess which has not been separately assured" of spiritualism's veracity. Despite ridicule by the public and in the press (in 1919 the *New York Times* went so far as to call his beliefs "pathetic"), Conan Doyle persisted, writing volume upon volume about spiritualism and touring the world to spread its gospel in lectures and talks. He considered it, he said, "the basis for all religious improvement in the future of the human race."

Sir Arthur Conan Doyle died of a heart attack in the summer of 1930. He was in full command of his literary powers until the end, publishing some of his finest Holmes stories as late as 1927 and the ambitious science-fiction novel *The Maracot Deep* the year before his passing. He was, and remains, one of Britain's most celebrated literary heroes.

The Collected Wit and Wisdom of Sherlock Holmes

On Crime:

The most commonplace crime is often the most mysterious because it presents no new or special features from which deductions may be drawn.

—*A Study in Scarlet*

You have heard me remark that the strangest and most unique things are very often connected not with the larger but with the smaller crimes, and occasionally, indeed, where there is room for doubt whether any positive crime has been committed.

—"The Red Headed League"

It's a wicked world, and when a clever man turns his brain to crime it is the worst of all.

—"The Adventure of the Speckled Band"

Crime is common. Logic is rare. Therefore it is upon the logic rather than upon the crime that you should dwell.

—"The Adventure of the Copper Beeches"

On Detection:

Detection is, or ought to be, an exact science, and should be treated in the same cold and unemotional manner.

—*The Sign of the Four*

Eliminate all other factors, and the one which remains must be the truth.

—*The Sign of the Four*

Nothing clears up a case so much as stating it to another person.

—"The Adventure of Silver Blaze"

Any truth is better than indefinite doubt.

—"The Adventure of the Yellow Face"

You know my method. It is founded upon the observance of trifles.

—"The Boscombe Valley Mystery"

I see no more than you, but I have trained myself to notice what I see.

—"The Adventure of the Blanched Soldier"

On Education:

Education never ends Watson. It is a series of lessons with the greatest for the last.

—"The Adventure of the Red Circle"

On Intelligence:

Some people without possessing genius have a remarkable power of stimulating it.

—*The Hound of the Baskervilles*

To the logician all things should be seen exactly as they are, and to underestimate one's self is as much a departure from truth as to exaggerate one's own powers.

—"The Adventure of the Greek Interpreter"

On London:

The lowest and vilest alleys in London do not present a more dreadful record of sin than does the smiling and beautiful countryside.

—"The Adventure of the Copper Beeches"

On Marriage:

Should I ever marry, Watson, I should hope to inspire my wife with some feeling which would prevent her from being walked off by a housekeeper when my corpse was lying within a few yards of her.

—*The Valley of Fear*

On Women:

I have never loved, Watson, but if I did and if the woman I loved had met such an end, I might act even as our lawless lion-hunter has done. Who knows?

—"The Adventure of the Devil's Foot"

Single ladies must live, and their passbooks are compressed diaries.

—"The Disappearance of Lady Frances Carfax"

On Nature:

One's ideas must be as broad as Nature if they are to interpret Nature.

—*A Study in Scarlet*

On Himself:

Out of my last 53 cases 49 have been given full credit to the police and the rest to me.

—"The Adventure of the Naval Treaty"

I never make exceptions. An exception disproves the rule.

—*The Sign of the Four*

My life is spent in one long effort to escape from the commonplaces of existence.

—"The Red Headed League"

I am an omnivorous reader with a strangely retentive memory for trifles.

—"The Adventure of the Lion's Mane"

No man lives or has ever lived who has brought the same amount of study and of natural talent to the detection of crime which I have done.

—*A Study in Scarlet*

On Life:

Life is infinitely stranger than anything which the mind of man could invent.

—"A Case of Identity"

What you do in this world is a matter of no consequence. . . . The question is, what can you make people believe that you have done.

—*A Study in Scarlet*

But there are always some lunatics about. It would be a dull world without them.

—"The Adventure of the Three Gables"

The Sherlock Holmes Canon

 n the sincere hope that this book will inspire readers to discover (or to reacquaint themselves with) Holmes's adventures, what follows is a complete list of the Sherlock Holmes short stories and novels.

THE SHORT STORIES

The Adventures of Sherlock Holmes (1891–92)

A Scandal in Bohemia

The Red-Headed League

A Case of Identity

The Boscombe Valley Mystery

The Five Orange Pips

The Man with the Twisted Lip

The Adventure of the Blue Carbuncle

The Adventure of the Speckled Band

The Adventure of the Engineer's Thumb

The Adventure of the Noble Bachelor

The Adventure of the Beryl Coronet

The Adventure of the Copper Beeches

The Memoirs of Sherlock Holmes (1892–93)

Silver Blaze

The Adventure of the Cardboard Box

The Adventure of the Yellow Face

The Adventure of the Stock-Broker's Clerk

The Adventure of the "Gloria Scott"

The Adventure of the Musgrave Ritual

The Adventure of the Reigate Squires

The Adventure of the Crooked Man

The Adventure of the Resident Patient

The Adventure of the Greek Interpreter

The Adventure of the Naval Treaty

The Final Problem

The Return of Sherlock Holmes (1903–4)

The Adventure of the Empty House

The Adventure of the Norwood Builder

The Adventure of the Dancing Men

The Adventure of the Solitary Cyclist

The Adventure of the Priory School

The Adventure of Black Peter

The Adventure of Charles Augustus Milverton

The Adventure of the Six Napoleons

The Adventure of the Three Students

The Adventure of the Golden Pince-Nez

The Adventure of the Missing Three-Quarter

The Adventure of the Abbey Grange

The Adventure of the Second Stain

His Last Bow (1908–17)

The Adventure of Wisteria Lodge

The Adventure of the Red Circle

The Adventure of the Bruce-Partington Plans

The Adventure of the Dying Detective

The Disappearance of Lady Frances Carfax

The Adventure of the Devil's Foot

His Last Bow

The Case of Sherlock Holmes (1921–27)

The Adventure of the Illustrious Client

The Adventure of the Blanched Soldier

The Adventure of the Mazarin Stone

The Adventure of the Three Gables

The Adventure of the Sussex Vampire

The Adventure of the Three Garridebs

The Problem of Thor Bridge

The Adventure of the Creeping Man

The Adventure of the Lion's Mane

The Adventure of the Veiled Lodger

The Adventure of Shoscombe Old Place

The Adventure of the Retired Colourman

THE NOVELS

A Study in Scarlet (1887)

The Sign of the Four (1890)

The Hound of the Baskervilles (1901)

The Valley of Fear (1914)

About the Author

Ransom Riggs has coauthored several books of what he likes to call "pop nonfiction," including the trivia-centric tomes *Scatterbrained* and *The Beginning of Everything*. He's a regular contributor to and blogger for *mental_floss* magazine, and when he's not unearthing fascinating-but-obscure miscellany, he's lying for a living as an award-winning filmmaker in Los Angeles, where he lives with his wife, Abbi. You can stalk him on the Web at www.ransomriggs.com.

Acknowledgments

In some semblance of chronological order, I have to thank John Green, who gave me my first nonfiction book-writing gig and introduced me to Mangesh Hattikudur, the steady and talented co-captain of the good ship *mental_floss*, who introduced me to Jason Rekulak, a very fine fellow and the editor of this book. I owe further debts to my agent, Kate Schafer Testerman; to my friend and tireless research assistant Anne Morrissy, without whom finishing this book in a timely and accurate manner would surely have been impossible; and to the generations of Sherlockian scholars whose excellent work made my job ever so much easier. Thanks also to Eugene Smith for his wonderful illustrations and to designer Doogie Horner. Finally, thanks to my lovely wife, Abbi, whose support means everything.

irreference \ir-ˈef-(ə-)rən(t)s\ *n* (2009)
   1 : irreverent reference
   2 : real information that also entertains or amuses

How-Tos. Quizzes. Instructions.
Recipes. Crafts. Jokes.
Trivia. Games. Tricks.
Quotes. Advice. Tips.

Learn something. Or not.

VISIT IRREFERENCE.COM
The New Quirk Books Web Site